PRAISE FOR *PARTY IN THE FRONT!*

"We are called to impact others; to feed the hungry, provide drink for the thirsty, and clothe those in need. This can't be done without a real understanding of those around us, and meeting people where they are in the midst of their lives. Jeff and Ty are leading us in a movement to love those around us, meet practical needs, and impact lives forever."

Paul Box, Co-Founder of Walk-In-Love, Inc., a local non-profit aiming to meet the practical needs of those living within ten minutes of someone's door.

"Having lived in LA for many years, I can tell you that city life is a lonely life. You really have to put yourself out there to feel whole. I love Jeff and Ty's idea to *Party in the Front!* and take on the problem of loneliness in a fun and practical way."

Michael O'Rourke, Founder of Sexy Hair

"The gift of hospitality makes the opening of other gifts possible; laughter, singing, shared meals and stories, shoulders to cry on, neighbors who pay attention. In short, community. Perhaps some of the answers to the world's problems are simpler than we thought. Perhaps those answers are right in front of us—in our own front yards. Thank you, Ty & Jeff!"

Kelly Kullberg, Founder of the Veritas Forum; Author of Finding God at Harvard *(Harper/Zondervan; IVP)*

"What a tremendously needed message! I so believe in this book and its articulation of the crying need of our society...and that is true community. Isolation is dangerous, and can cause one to quickly spiral downward. Conversely, when we have others to share our burdens, true friendship and fellowship take place, and that is life giving and life changing. However as this book articulates, we must act with intention for this to happen, as it seems everything sets out to prevent it. As Jeff and Ty make clear, this intention will provide us with an understanding of how precious, how beautiful, and how crucial community is. Let this book be a catalyst in motivating you to be the difference maker in your family, neighborhood, and wherever you go. Allow this book to be the inspiration that changes your relationships and leaves a legacy of blessed memories and cherished relationships for life. The Bible makes these sentiments clear in Ecclesiastes 4:9-12 and Galatians 6:2."

Wade McHargue, Author of Elijah Generation, *Pastor*

"In a world that often feels fragmented and disconnected, this book overflows with genuine hope—not wishful thinking, but the kind of grounded, biblical assurance that speaks to our deep longing for connection. Ty and Jeff write with clarity, conviction, and compassion, offering timeless truths that can transform lives, families, and communities. I have the joy of knowing both of these men and their families personally, and their daily lives reflect the very message they share here. Their commitment to Christ and to cultivating meaningful connection has shaped my own family and those around us. If you're yearning for a sense of belonging or searching for practical ways to build community with purpose, this book will inspire and equip you to do just that."

Eryn Lynum, Bible teacher, Host of Nat Theo Podcast, *and author of* The Nature of Rest: What the Bible and Creation Teach Us About Sabbath Living

"In a day when we barely know our neighbors and so many carry the quiet burden of loneliness, this book may offer just what we need: compelling, practical ways to cultivate relationships and reflect the love of Jesus right where we are. I hope many front yards and homes become hubs of community because of this book."

Scott Hubbard, Managing Editor of Desiring God, Lay Pastor at All People's Church in Minneapolis

"We love the *Party in the Front!* idea. One summer afternoon, we built a simple bike ramp in our front yard that quickly became a neighborhood attraction as kids from around the block started showing up, wanting to take a turn trying it out. That evening, our son wanted to invite all the parents to come watch a bike "show," and with some simple invitations, texts, and word of mouth, the families arrived with lawn chairs in tow, creating an impromptu block party right on our front lawn. As the kids (and some of the dads!) took turns jumping their bikes, the rest of the families naturally fell into conversations about family updates and deepened relationships. What began as a simple afternoon project with our kids transformed into a gathering place for our neighbors where we could share our lives and faith with people who might never have stepped foot inside our church. These front yard connections continue to open doors and create meaningful connections with our kids while also modeling for them how to intentionally connect with those God has placed in our lives."

Jason and Wendy Valderrama, CEOs of their Neighborhood Bike Ramp

"Party In The Front! This stuff matters. A few years back, we made a shift as a family. We stopped waiting for community to find us and started building it ourselves. We kicked off something called SUNDay Sundae. Every Sunday, we opened up our home. We'd invite the neighborhood, people from church, folks in the community—whoever wanted to come. Some weeks two people showed up, other weeks, 20. Didn't matter. The ice cream was good, but the people were better. That little tradition changed everything. Opening our door opened our hearts. It helped us to stop thinking just about ourselves and start thinking more about others. It wasn't perfect or polished—but it was real. And real is what we all need more of."

Jordan Abaroa, CEO of his Neighborhood
SUNDay Sundae

"I lived on the upper level of my condominium complex next to Ty and his young family for a couple of years. It was an absolute joy every morning for me to look out and see their children playing on the sidewalk between our buildings or out on their front patio. They would talk to the other neighbors and myself as we went to and from work, and it was a real treat to hear about their little adventures each day. One thing led to another and we eventually shared some meals together. We even held a baking class in their kitchen one day since I owned my own bakery for many years. The sense of community that was created among all of us resulted in a real feeling of togetherness throughout our neighborhood. Thank you for writing this book!"

Melonie Fusilier, Former Neighbor of the
Dannenbring Family

PARTY IN THE FRONT!

OVERCOME LONELINESS
AND BUILD COMMUNITY
RIGHT WHERE YOU ARE

TY DANNENBRING + JEFF DILLON

Story BUILDERS PRESS

To our wives and families,

Thank you for your unending love and support - and for helping us bring the party to the front in our everyday lives. None of this would be possible without you.

To the lonely and all those on a mission to build community,

This book is for you.

FOREWORD

Ty's idea for this book has resulted in new friendships and a stronger community in our Ohio suburb.

In April of 2023, an exciting musical duo, The Lindsley Brothers (Jon and Trey), were touring. I contacted them to see if they'd be passing through our city, Columbus, Ohio. They weren't performing here, but kindly said that they could make it work. Our home would be the venue.

It can still snow in Ohio, in April, so my husband and I first envisioned a small gathering of family and friends, either inside by the piano and a fire, or under tents in the back yard.

As the day arrived, a hopeful taste of springtime was evident. Redbuds and daffodils peaked out after a long winter. We pulled furniture out of the garage, and set up out back, away from the neighbors—out back where no strangers would wander in, and where we had more control of the situation, I suppose.

Then I remembered Ty's idea—Party in the Front! But we hadn't removed all the leaves and branches, and the tree swing was wobbly, and we hadn't planted, and it was a bit chilly, and besides, who would come on a weekday evening to hear a then-unknown band, and so on. My mind wandered.

I ran the front yard idea by my creative, adventurous, and people-loving 9-year-old granddaughter, Sydney. She knew a few of their songs and she caught the vision. She very excitedly said, "Let's invite the whole neighborhood!" I sent out texts. She quickly hand made 30 invitations, recruited cousins, and then we all went door to door throughout the neighborhood. "Please come to our front yard—in 20 minutes! We have hot dogs and T-shirts signed by the Lindsley Brothers!" No one had heard of the Texas-based duo—but neither could they turn down her enthusiastic offer.

Within an hour, our intimate gathering of 20 became a party of 50 people in our front yard. I spotted some of our grandkids perched in a pear tree, taking it all in. Neighbors, some of whom we had never met, gathered around fire pits introducing themselves, eating hot dogs and ice cream, and singing along to the songs of James Taylor, Dan Fogelberg, the Lindsleys and more.

That night, new and deeper friendships began to blossom in our neighborhood. We invited several strangers to our weekly "campfire" Bible/dinner club. We celebrated the end of a bitter winter and arrival of spring. We had a blast. The Lindsley Brothers drove off the next day, hopefully encouraged by this spur-of-the-moment decision to party in the front!

Last year, Jon Lindsley auditioned for American Idol and, though, more famous now, the duo returned to our front yard again last spring. My niece, Sydney, was ceremoniously declared the President of The Lindsley Brothers Ohio Fan Club. She and her cousins once again invited the entire neighborhood to the party—"see you in 20 minutes!"

New friends on the street now host their own creative versions of parties in the front, including one family's big-screen movie nights. Existing neighborhood traditions continue—like setting out Christmas luminaries, and potluck dinner nights.

The gift of hospitality so often inspires others to offer the same—to pay it forward. So many, in turn, find themselves sharing laughter, music, meals, and stories with neighbors who were previously strangers. They recognize the impact of offering shoulders to cry on, and taking the time to really listen. In short—they recognize the power of community.

Perhaps some of the answers to the world's problems are simpler—and much closer—than we think. Perhaps they are right in front of our eyes—in our own front yards.

Thank you, Ty & Jeff!

Kelly Monroe Kullberg
Author of Finding God at Harvard *(Harper/Zondervan; IVP)*
Co-author of A Faith & Culture Devotional *(Zondervan)*
General Secretary of the American Association of Evangelicals (AAE)
Founder of the Veritas Forum

TABLE OF CONTENTS

INTRODUCTION

From the moment we enter this world, we search for connections with other people. In fact, scientists believe that babies begin to recognize and imitate their mothers' facial expressions within seven hours of birth!

Throughout childhood we long for close friends, hope to be included with the group at the playground, and dread being picked last in kickball.

Later, during adolescence, we care deeply about our friend groups, about being recognized for achievements, or being accepted into the college of our dreams. In many ways, growing up feels like one giant game of "where do I fit in?"

Those feelings don't go away when we become adults. They just look and feel different. Despite the life changes we experience, community and connection remain a pressing need for all of us. As adults, we long to be appreciated in a thriving workplace, and to be rewarded for the gifts and experience we bring to a cause. We feel left out when we don't receive a dinner invitation extended to the rest of our friends and coworkers.

Why? Simply put, it's because we were not intended to exist in isolation. We were designed to be with each other—to need, know, and be welcomed in by one another.

In the dictionary, community is defined as "a social group of any size whose members reside in a specific locality, share government, and/or often have a common cultural and historical heritage."[1]

In simpler terms, a community is a group of people with shared interests. Throughout our lives we all experience being members of communities—our workplaces, our churches, our friend groups, etc. But perhaps the most obvious community space is the one most overlooked—our neighborhoods.

For the vast majority of us, neighborhoods are our primary communities. And in these vitally important settings, it is only normal for us to want to connect—to know, and to be known by, fellow members. Yet it seems harder than ever to develop meaningful relationships with others in this increasingly disconnected world. And getting to knowing our neighbors in the 21st century is perhaps harder than it has ever been. We're too busy, or assume they don't want to be bothered. Still, all of us have a deep desire and innate need for community.

COMMUNITY IS CORE

Community is core to what it means to be human. Followers of Jesus recognize this fundamental truth—indeed, commandment—which is found throughout the New and Old Testaments. In the first chapter of the first book of Scripture, God gives breath to the first man—Adam. He is placed reverently in the Garden of Eden, and all seems right with the world.

Except...it's not. Something is missing. Here's what we read in Genesis 1:

"Then the Lord God said, 'It is not good that the man should be alone; I will make him a helper fit for him.' The man gave names to all livestock and to the birds of the heavens and to every beast of the field. But for Adam there was not found a helper fit for him. So the Lord God caused a deep sleep to fall upon the man, and while he slept took one of his ribs and closed up its place with flesh. And the rib that the Lord God had taken from the man he made into a woman and brought her to the man. Then the man said, 'This at last is bone of my bones and flesh of my flesh; she shall be called Woman, because she was taken out of Man.'" (Genesis 1:18, 20-23)

Pause, and ask yourself, "If I had everything I wanted, lived in a place I loved, and did exactly what I was meant to do, would I ever really need anyone else?" God answers this question in the first sentence of the verse: "It is not good that the man should be alone." This incredible story at the dawn of creation makes the answer crystal clear. "Yes."

Even Adam, in this flawless setting—prior to the blemish of sin entering the world—felt incomplete without someone at his side. He *needed* another human being—flesh of his flesh. Right there in the Garden, God has graced us with the incredible gift of community: relationships with other human beings; people to know and be known by; loved ones to help; friends with whom to walk, talk, and relate; partners with whom to figure out the world.

This need doesn't end with the story of Genesis 1. It continues throughout all of Scripture; Abraham's desire for a child, the formation of God's chosen people of Israel, and the many festivals and feasts Israel would celebrate in community. It continues with the birth of God's only son, Jesus, into a human family; with the assembling of the twelve disciples among whom he shared his faith and beliefs; and with the birth of the Church family, created to reveal God's love and truth through the members' relationships with each other and the rest of the world. You could say that the story of Scripture is, in many ways, first and foremost about relationships; God's relationship with man, man's broken relationship with God and the restoration of that relationship, and man's relationship with others.

All of this underscores the premise of our book. Community is vital. We were never intended to live life as lone rangers, trying to figure it out on our own. We need one another. We need to be a part of something bigger than ourselves—to be welcomed into a group that says to us, "We see you. We care about you. We accept you." Every day, we find ourselves in the same spaces as countless fellow human beings who experience exactly the same need. The fact is, we live in a world where—increasingly and far too often—our need for community is simply not met.

Just as with Adam in the Garden, it is not good for man to be alone.

This truth presents to each and every one of us an amazing opportunity. We live next to, work with, and experience life alongside countless people with the same powerful desire—to connect.

Overcoming loneliness and pursuing community starts with each of us. It starts with the recognition of these truths and a willingness to reach out to those around us.

Each of us can build community right where we are, and have a really good time doing it.

LOVE YOUR NEIGHBOR

Let's be honest. This idea may feel unfamiliar and seem a little scary. Getting to know my neighbors? Being known by them? Opening my life to them? Yikes! These things don't come naturally to most of us. We'll explore the reasons for this later in the book.

To make matters worse, we live in a world that is increasingly working against us in the pursuit of connectedness. We live in homes separated by thick walls and tall fences. We park our cars in garages and close the automatic doors behind us the moment we're inside.

We engage with technology and the Internet to make us "feel" as though we are "a part." We have a culture that is becoming more polarized politically and socially. In 2020, we dealt with a global pandemic that required us to stay at least six feet away from each other!

In 2023, the US Surgeon General declared an "Epidemic of Loneliness and Isolation."[2] To summarize, the Surgeon General's report found that nearly half of adults in the US experience some level of loneliness on a regular basis.

Loneliness is nothing new to our world, but it is certainly on the rise. And considering the profound impact this feeling can have on us, the stakes are clearly high.

Our goal in writing this book is to encourage the Church to love our neighbors well. People are often drawn to the saving power of Christ through the love that they experience from his followers.

If you are parched for community, we will show you that the living water is to be found in the community of Jesus' Church. You will find spiritual life through Jesus, and relational life through the Church.

If we want our neighbors to know Jesus, we must first get to know them. This is at the heart of the life and teachings of Jesus:

"And you shall love the Lord your God with all your heart and with all your soul and with all your mind and with all your strength. You shall love your neighbor as yourself. There is no other commandment greater than these." (Mark 12:30-31)

It's fundamental to who we are and the mission we've been given.

However, the need for—and the opportunity to create—community isn't limited to Christians. Every one of us, regardless of faith or tradition, shares a deep need for loving and lasting relationships. Our relational connections play a huge part in maintaining mental and emotional health in a lonely and disconnected age.

OPEN DOORS

As we'll see, the challenges are great. But so are the opportunities. Life as we know it has not always been this way.

In this book, we look back at the way things used to be in order to help us understand the demise of community. We reveal how the Gospel heals and transforms these wounds. We give you practical ideas and introduce narratives to inspire you to take your first steps toward restoring community within your neighborhood, and recognizing the importance of creating and nurturing a meaningful Gospel-centered community right where you live. Perhaps you'll find out that it's not as difficult or scary as you thought. All it takes is a willingness to step just a little bit outside your comfort zone. Open your door. Invite your neighbors over for a party in the front...and maybe throw in some popsicles or a corn hole set.

With a few simple steps, you can transform your home and neighborhood from one of isolation to one of connectedness and community. You really can.

Building community right where you are is possible. And it is powerful.

It's time to take loneliness by the horns.

It's time to restore community in style.

It's time to *Party in the Front!*

CHAPTER 1
PARTY IN THE FRONT!

"Jesus is handing out God's party invitations.
They read: 'You're invited to my party in the new
creation. Come as you are.'" —Tim Chester

STORIES FROM THE FRONT

Ty: A few years back, I experienced God's grace thanks to a milk cow and a neighbor who needed a workout buddy.

I was single and at a crossroads in my life. I was experiencing depression and anxiety in a soul-crushing way. I thought my heart was going to explode out of my chest. I couldn't get out of bed. And I was convinced that the world would be much safer if I didn't exist—a state of mind in which I thought I would never, ever find myself.

Put simply, I needed help.

As part of my healing process, I moved in with a family from my church who lived on a farm. And while I was living there, I was expected to help. So I was given the

---

7:00am shift to milk the dairy cow. (And yes, the cow did have a typical name like Bessie or something like that).

As silly as it sounds, it was exactly what I needed. My soul longed for hope and purpose and this dusty old dairy cow provided me a reason to get out of bed, to be around people, to move forward. I thank God for that cow, and for the family who provided a place of refuge for me when I desperately needed it.

As time went on at the farm, I added running to my daily routine. While out one day, I met a neighbor about my age who needed help training for admission to The Citadel (The Military College of South Carolina). Our workouts were nothing fancy. We used some dumbbells and old tires, and trained on his front lawn. Having been a college athlete,

I was able to serve and encourage him on his journey, and having a faithful friend helped my soul heal in a hard season of my life.

At my lowest point, what I needed most wasn't a grand vision, a personal breakthrough, or even a triumphant success. As it turned out, I needed to be reminded of God's grace. I needed to take the focus off of myself, milk a cow and serve a neighbor.

In short, I needed community.

COWS ARE A BIG DEAL THESE DAYS. HAVE YOU NOTICED?

Just take a trip to your local home store or search online for popular interior artwork. You'll see there's a real cow trend going on. You might even call it a moo-vement. (That's the worst joke in this book, we promise.)

But it's true. Cows are cool. And there's one cow in particular that truly stands out from the herd: the Highland. You've seen photos of them, no doubt. These big, beautiful, furry specimens of Scottish descent are loved by farmers for their ability to thrive in varied climates, thanks to their crazy-thick outer coat, which grows more dense in winter and sheds in the spring. They are well-known for their stately, long horns, which can grow up to four feet in length, tip-to-tip.

BUSINESS IN THE BACK, PARTY IN THE FRONT

It's impossible not to smile when you see a picture of a Highland. That epic, eye-catching, mullet-styled fur is very reminiscent of the haircut worn by trendy 1980s high schoolers. Flip those mullets back to front and you wind up with something that resembles the look of the Highland cow.

Right about now, you're likely asking yourself, "What in the world does the Highland cow have to do with community?" Good question!

These amazing creatures bring smiles to the faces of everyone. They capture our attention, and draw us in. Perhaps we should take a few cues from the Highland. By taking ourselves a little less seriously we encourage others to do the same—making both them and us more comfortable. We can truly and freely be who we were made to be.

We can absolutely spark a moo-vement in our neighborhoods and communities that has a positive impact, connects our lives, and fights back against the epidemic of loneliness that has swept through our world.

It all starts with bringing the party to the front.

THE POWER OF THE FRONT PORCH

There is something unique about the front porch. It's where we welcome guests to our homes. It's the gateway between "out there" and "in here." It's the first thing people notice about a dwelling. It's where we might hang the American flag or a Denver Broncos banner, or set out a fun welcome mat that says, "Hi. I'm Mat." (These exist by the way, and they're awesome.)

But, what if you don't have a front porch? Perhaps you live in an apartment or condo, or in a neighborhood built in the mid 1900s when air conditioning and television were gaining popularity and people began spending more time indoors.

Not a problem! You may not have a front porch, but I'm guessing you almost certainly have a front door or stoop or portal—in short, a space that serves as an entry point to your home.

And here's the thing: This space is powerful.

It's powerful because your front porch/entryway/door is seen by everyone who passes your home. While your neighbors may not have seen your kitchen sink, your bathroom (thankfully), your backyard, or the inside of your garage, they have to see your entryway—it's the public face of your home, and your secret weapon for building community.

It's not about making this space awesome (although there are certainly many fun and creative ways to do so). It's about bringing something from the inside...outside. It's about taking what's closed off and opening it up to others. This is the power of the front porch. You can't hide there. You can't close the garage door over it. The front of your home is there for the world to see.

How amazing would it be to use that space, not as a barrier between our neighbors and us, but rather as a gathering spot—a place of connectedness and caring and laughter and prayer? What kind of impact do you suppose that would make in your neighborhood?

WHERE THE PARTY'S AT

We all love parties. Well, at least we did when we were kids. As adults, the thought of a big party may sometimes send us searching, with lightening speed, for the "no" response on the RSVP email. Because, to many of us, a great party is simply a summer BBQ, gathering to watch the big game with friends, or engaging a small group of people in deep conversation over a warm cup of coffee.

Fact is, any get-together qualifies as a party if it's fun, meaningful, and shared with neighbors, friends and/or family.

You may be surprised to learn that partying is a Biblical concept—a strongly encouraged Biblical concept, no less.

This might sound strange, considering what we typically think of as a party in our culture. However, the parties we read about in Scripture don't qualify as displays of debauchery. Instead, the Bible describes a very different picture of a party. And—you guessed it—it's all about community.

Celebrations were common in the Old Testament. In Deuteronomy 14, God commands the Israelites to eat and drink and rejoice together before him in light of His goodness.

Later in the Old Testament, a priest named Ezra reads the Law of Moses before a sullen people who were convicted of the many ways in which they had broken God's laws, and afterward makes a surprising declaration. The people are instructed to rejoice and celebrate the Feast of Tabernacles with great gladness, despite initially weeping upon hearing the weight of the law—essentially, that following God's commandments should bring joy, not sorrow.

They are told to *"Go and enjoy choice food and sweet drinks, and send some to those who have nothing prepared. This day is holy to our Lord. Do not grieve, for the joy of the Lord is your strength."* (Nehemiah 8:10)

What do the people do in response to this call? Party! They celebrate out of worship and gratitude for God and his Word.

In the New Testament, we find Jesus' very first miracle taking place at a wedding (John 2). We read about Jesus repeatedly feasting with people of many backgrounds—much to the chagrin of the religious teachers of the day (Luke 5). Jesus used many wedding and feast analogies in his teachings, often citing the parable of the great banquet, in which he compares the Kingdom of God to a party you definitely want to attend (Luke 14).

The Bible points to the ultimate, party-to-end-all-parties that will take place in Heaven one day. This party, referred to as the Wedding Feast of the Lamb, will take place when God's people are united with Jesus for all of eternity. It will be massive. And it will be beautiful.

Check out the heavenly scene described by John, the author of Revelation:

"Then I heard what seemed to be the voice of a great multitude, like the roar of many waters and like the sound of mighty peals of thunder, crying out, 'Hallelujah! For the Lord our God the Almighty reigns. Let us rejoice and exult and give him the glory, for the marriage of the Lamb has come, and his Bride has made herself ready; it was granted her to clothe herself with fine linen, bright and pure—for the fine linen is the righteous deeds of the saints.' And the angel said to me, 'Write this: Blessed are those who are invited to the marriage supper of the Lamb.'" (Revelation 19:6-9a)

The "Bride" referred to is the Church—God's people, who have been saved by grace through faith in Jesus Christ. What happens in Heaven? A huge celebration with multitudes in attendance, partying with the Lamb himself—Jesus.

Like that Tim Chester quote says, Jesus is generously handing out invitations to this party-to-end-all parties. God wants you to be there. Jesus has welcomed us to join him for this celebration. As we'll see, that's exactly what Jesus does throughout Scripture. He invites us to experience joy and life and community with him.

There's no denying it—partying is God's idea! He invites his people to celebrate for good and Godly reasons—to eat good food, drink good drinks, and to do it not out of gluttony, but out of gratitude for him and what he's done.

To party is to be grateful.

To party is to declare the goodness of God.

To party is to welcome other people into a place of joy and gratitude.

To party is to pursue community.

This is why there is a deep sense of satisfaction and happiness when we gather for birthday parties, Fourth of July BBQs, children's play dates, a season finale watch party—all these events enable us to celebrate life together.

But here's the dilemma. Most often, these assemblies take place either inside our homes or in our backyards. And, there's nothing wrong with that. Typically, our backyards are more conducive to BBQs. And let's face it, inviting a group to a party in your driveway does seem a little bizarre.

What's more, most of our parties and gatherings are with our friends, families, and those we know well. This makes sense. It's wonderful to spend time with those we know and love.

But think about this for a moment. What might it look like to plan a gathering in the front of your home? To barbecue in the front yard instead of the back? To have a cup of coffee with a friend on your front porch instead of in the kitchen? To simply make yourself available for interactions with neighbors as they pass?

Here's what happens when you take this important first step toward creating community: You open yourself up to people with whom you normally wouldn't connect. Your gathering/conversation/meal is no longer an "us" get-together. It is now an open invitation to the entire neighborhood.

This is what it looks like to party in the front. You allow the people in your immediate surroundings to see you and interact with you. You are letting them know that even though there's a door and some drywall separating you from them, your life and heart are open to them right there on your front porch. It doesn't take a dramatic change to begin connecting with your neighbors. All it takes is being available.

So if it's that easy, why don't we all do it? Why does it seem a lot harder in reality than in theory? It turns out there are a lot of factors working against us when it comes to building community. Some have to do with the way we're shaped by our cultures and environments, and by the age in which we live. Some are the result of thousands of years of human history. But some of the greatest obstacles to creating community live within you.

THE JOURNEY

We're going to take a journey together in this book. First, we'll take a look at where we've been and how our culture has attempted to create connectedness through personal and professional relationships. We'll examine the strengths and the pitfalls of those seemingly more-communal days.

After that, we'll see where things went wrong, not just in the world but, more importantly, in ourselves. This perspective will provide a better understanding of why so many barriers to community still exist.

But we won't dwell on that for long. Because we'll find that there is great hope for us and the world through the message of the Gospel, and that this good news has the power to transform everything we know about relationships and community.

Finally, we'll leave you with a vision of the impact you can make right where you live. We'll also give you some fun and practical ways to begin the process of creating community with the people God has placed in your life.

We were moved to write this book because we have seen the possibility and power of community. We believe all of us have a calling and an ability to make an eternal impact by taking small steps toward the people in our sphere of influence.

You can do this. You can be like the Highland. You can put smiles on the faces of others as you reveal your willingness to be seen, known, and understood.

You can make a lasting impact in your world. You can start a ripple effect that brings hope to people near and far by simply reflecting your spiritual beliefs.

The keys to community are already in your pocket, just waiting to unlock unlimited potential and possibilities.

CHAPTER 2

WHERE WE'VE BEEN

"Community connectedness is not just about warm, fuzzy tales of civic triumph...social capital makes an enormous difference in our lives. It makes us smarter, healthier, safer...and better able to govern a just and stable democracy." –Robert Putnam

---

STORIES FROM THE FRONT

Jeff: It was a simple, rusty old swing with a tattered, yellow cushion. It hung from my grandparents' front porch on the west side of their two-story house in the small northern Colorado town of Eaton. That swing was where you'd find my grandfather, Grampy Don as we called him, just about any day of the week.

As a kid, I remember pulling up to my grandparents' home and seeing Grampy Don on that front porch swing—practically every time. In fact, if we arrived and didn't see him out there, we got a little worried. Where in the world could he be, if not on the front porch?

Grampy Don sat on the front porch while I played with my brother and my cousins. He sat there when, as a teenager, I mowed the lawn. And, at 89 years of age, he sat there before walking to the car to go to the hospital. Sadly, he never made it back to his front porch. But I like to picture him in Heaven, surveying those golden streets from his favorite swing.

As I look back, I realize that my grandfather wasn't just choosing to sit there because it was comfortable. Frankly, there were many more comfortable places to sit in his home. I realize now how important that swing was to him. From that spot he could see, hear, and interact daily with passers-by. Positioned in the center of Eaton, right across from the city park and just down the street from the school, Grampy Don had a front row seat to the comings and goings of friends and neighbors.

Even though my grandfather (a WWII veteran who parachuted into France during the battle of Normandy) wasn't exactly a "people person," he would always wave and say hello. Over decades in that house, Grampy Don got to know just about everyone in the neighborhood. And they knew him. He heard stories of babies born, marriages ended, friendships restored, and a community growing and changing. Grampy Don built community in his neighborhood simply by sitting on the front porch.

It's incredible how simple it can be to connect with your neighbors. All it takes is being present. My grandfather didn't plan a neighborhood picnic or make balloon animals for the kids at the park. He was just...there. Available. Friendly. It changed something about their neighborhood— and his legacy.

A SIMPLER TIME

Grampy Don was a member of a very challenged generation during a very difficult time in America's history. He was born into a still young and growing country. In the early 1900s, American culture was one of great social participation. The United States was a melting pot of cultures, with immigrants, worldwide, flocking to the country for economic opportunities.

As the country navigated the difficulties of World War I, the Great Depression, and World War II, American culture was shaped by shared ideals and values. Particularly in the 1940s, following World War II, the desire for a strong and vibrant America was palpable.

This vibrancy, a result of the post-war economic boom resulted in average Americans becoming far more affluent than they likely ever imagined, and certainly more well-off than their parents or grandparents. They had opportunities to travel, purchase homes, attend college, or even buy farms. It was time for them to create space to dream and grow.[3]

Over 40 million post-World War II Americans moved from cities and farmlands to the suburbs between 1940 and 1960. In search of a more stable, sustainable life beyond the hustle and bustle of major cities, people were getting married, having kids, and settling down in new and neatly designed neighborhoods. The 1940s Baby Boom made history. Our parents wouldn't have existed without it. And neither would we. Thanks Grandma and Grandpa!

Along with so many people moving into these carefully designed, coordinated communities, there came a new shift in 20th-century American culture: an embracing of life lived together, and a growing desire to raise kids in the same way as like-minded friends and neighbors. Now established in homes and intent on living the American dream in the suburbs, Americans gravitated toward social interaction and neighborhood relationships. It became a natural outflow of the new, post-war American ideal.

Levittown, New York, was the first—and, perhaps, most famous—example of the suburbia phenomenon. After the war, this suburban haven was built strictly for veterans. Homes in Levittown rented for $60 a month. In the years to follow, the population of this brand-new town swelled to over 80,000 people.

Levittown residents were seeking not only to escape city life: They were looking for community. As one early Levittown citizen remarked, "There wasn't anything we wouldn't do for each other—babysit, drive a neighbor somewhere, maybe help out with a mortgage payment someone couldn't meet."[4]

With neighborhoods like Levittown popping up across the country, there was a newfound sense of what people could build and become...together. Doesn't that sound awesome?

Well, yes...but while it is easy to look back with fondness, or even envy, over the way things were, we also have to be honest about the failures of "the good old days."

The truth is, there was a dark side to this suburban sprawl as well. Racial prejudice played a large part in the design and growth of these suburbs. For decades, Levittown would not sell homes to people of color. In fact, part of the appeal of the suburbs for many was just how racially homogenous it was.

We look back in dismay at facts like these, but it made sense to many at the time. Why not create communities where people are similar, houses are similar, and life is similar? This seemed like a beautiful blueprint for creating genuine community. In these communities, where everyone looks and lives similarly, and is striving for the same things, what's not to love?

While we may not realize it, this is the cultural idea of community that we often look back on endearingly. But if we're being honest, the cracks that existed in that seemingly golden era of American community were major ones. And those cracks only widened as time went on.

A CHANGING CULTURE

Change is inevitable, and certainly not always bad. But there is no question that there have been transformations in our society that have not been for the better. These shifts have made it harder for us to connect with each other than, perhaps, ever before.

The day when being a connected, committed part of your neighborhood community was common seems to be long gone. In its place, a growing sense of independence, disconnection, and distrust has emerged. Western society has undergone major shifts over the past couple of generations.

Midway through the 20th century, American culture was developing in ways that would eventually splinter neighbor-to-neighbor connections. Restaurants began popping up. The music industry exploded (Elvis Presley made his world debut with *That's All Right* in 1954). And watching television became the norm for many American families. In 1950, about 20% of Americans had a television in their homes. By 1960, that number had jumped to 90%![5]

While these developments didn't threaten neighborhood communities in and of themselves, it was clear that they were indications of cultural changes on the horizon. In his book, *Bowling Alone*, Robert D. Putnam breaks down the shifts in American society that began to accelerate beginning in the 1970s. Some of those shifts are clearly demonstrated by the following facts:

- The number of Americans who had friends over for dinner at least twice a month decreased from 50% in 1975 to 40% in 1995.

- During that same time frame, the number of Americans who went to a friend's house during a previous week for any reason dropped from 40% to 25%.

- Card playing rose in popularity in post-WWII American culture, but by the 1990s the number of people playing card games with friends and neighbors was declining by 25 million per year. We're guessing Solitaire gained popularity at about the same time.

- According to the General Social Survey, between 1974 and 1988, the amount of time Americans spent with a neighbor fell by about a third among married people, and by 50% among single adults.[6]

This is just a very small sampling of the cultural changes that took place from the 1950s through the early 1990s. It was as if the ground was beginning to move underneath us, whether we realized it or not.

THE FINAL STRAW

These shifts all occurred prior to the invention that would change the trajectory of life as we knew it—that's right, the Internet.

As the World Wide Web became accessible to everyone in the late 1990s and early 2000s, *everything* changed—and did so at warp speed. The idea of community became threatened as never before.

From 1996—as the Internet was first becoming a "thing"— to the turn of the century five years later, 361 million people worldwide gained access to the Internet (and countless American teenagers tied up their landlines while chatting with their friends on AOL.[7] Our hands are raised.

Certainly, there have been benefits from the advancement of the Internet. We have access to incredible amounts of information. It is now effortless to communicate with people over long distances, even halfway around the world. And, of course, we have *Angry Birds* and *Candy Crush*!

Yet, in so many ways, the Internet created more challenges to community than benefits. Suddenly, it became far more possible to feel like you had community—and lots of it— without actually *experiencing* that community.

When Facebook came on the scene in 2004, the ability to connect with friends through social media felt like a game-changer. Over time, the number of these online friends grew, but so did the sinking suspicion that we weren't *actually* friends with most of them.

Oh sure, maybe we were close at one point, but how many of these online acquaintances did we *truly* have a relationship with? For these two writers, it was very few (don't reveal this to our 20-year-old selves. They'd be devastated).

In essence, the Internet—and social media in particular—allows us to have "friends" without much (if any) real, personal connection or investment. Sure, we get to see their photos. We share curated pieces of our lives with them. And in a split second, we log off and leave them behind. Does that sound like a meaningful relationship?

The Internet and social media revolutions have had another unintended downside. They have created an environment in which we can prune and shape our idea of community, without being obligated to interact with diverse voices, cultures, and perspectives.

If I don't like your political takes on Facebook, I mute you. If I don't like the philosophy behind your posts, I unfollow you. On the other hand, if I agree with you, and if what you say affirms what I believe or want, I follow, like, and share! Thumbs up, baby!

Over time, our culture has become more and more acclimated to what is now called echo chambers, sites on which we feel more comfortable with the realities and ideas that agree with our own, and more and more uncomfortable with anything that seems opposed. Social media isn't just a place where this *can* happen. These websites and apps are created specifically for the purpose of putting us in a nice, comfortable bubble shared with people whose ideas are most aligned with our own. Instead of expanding our world, they narrow it by identifying subjects, obsessions, and prejudices that make us tick as individuals. And by focusing on them, their significance becomes magnified in our lives—the ultimate echo chambers.

As the online education non-profit GCF Global explains, "A social media echo chamber is when one experiences a biased, tailored media experience that eliminates opposing viewpoints and differing voices. Due to social media algorithms that ensure we only see media that fits our preferences, we have found ourselves in a comfortable, self-confirming feed."[8]

Not only do we have physical and social barriers that prevent us from establishing meaningful person to person community, but algorithms are now accomplishing the same result worldwide: the homogenization of community via a carefully and cautiously-curated concept which encourages us to be skeptical of anyone who looks or lives differently.

Call it a modern, digital version of Levittown.

Put simply, we've moved a long, long way from Grampy Don's simple front porch swing. Our ability to engage with strangers, and to understand those who look and live differently, has suffered greatly.

The result of these cultural and societal changes? A whole lot of disconnected, lonely people. You don't have to look far to see the negative effects of these cultural changes on community and relationships.

The US Surgeon General's 2023 report titled "Our Epidemic of Loneliness and Isolation" outlines some of the most eye-opening effects:

- Nearly one out of two adults in the US reports experiencing some level of loneliness, defined as a distressing experience that results from perceived isolation or inadequate meaningful connections.

- Around 57% of Americans know only some of their neighbors. However, 17% of Americans know none of their neighbors. This number jumps to 23% for young adults under age 30.

- Among those who do know at least some of their neighbors, 58% say they never have meaningful connections with them.[9]

And these realities don't just affect people emotionally or relationally. There are very real health risks associated with the lack of meaningful community.

The Surgeon General's report found that a lack of social connection is more dangerous to our health than smoking up to 15 cigarettes daily!

In other words, people could literally be dying from loneliness.

A CHANGING CHURCH

As Christians, it's easy to point a finger at the culture "out there" and cite all the things wrong with it. But the truth is, many (if not all) of the problems we see in the world can often be found inside the church as well.

This is certainly true when it comes to the phenomenon of weakening community. Few institutions have suffered more in terms of community erosion in recent decades.

Just look at the numbers. According to Gallup, US church membership sat at 70% or higher from 1937 (shortly before the beginning of WWII) through 1976, decreasing only slightly to 68% from the 1970s to the 1990s.[10]

From the 1990s on, the drop in church attendance is stunning—from 70% in 1998 to 50% in 2018, just two decades later. By 2020, that number fell below 50% for the first time.

The week-to-week attendance numbers are even more startling. According to Pew Research, just 20% of Americans regularly attend church. A majority of Americans (57%) say they rarely or never attend.[11]

The global COVID pandemic which entered the American conversation in January, 2020, only accelerated many of these changes, with 16% of American Christians who attended church pre-pandemic no longer attending at all.

Another reason for these dramatic drops in church attendance is the increasing number of Americans who no longer claim any religious affiliation.[12] Regardless of the reasons, there are fewer and fewer people going to church these days, a place that has historically been a primary source of community.

In fact, research done in 2023 showed that 57% of Americans believe the church has either no impact or a negative impact on the community.[13] That means there are millions of people in our country today who believe church is harmful to people. Ouch.

These statistics leave us with the harsh reality that the church, as it has historically functioned in this country, is no longer a source of community for most Americans. The fact that fewer people are attending church is only part of the problem. It's also—and maybe even more significantly—the reality that many people who do attend church aren't finding genuine community there either.

This is where we get into some difficult terrain. We love the church, and so does Jesus. Jesus tells Peter *"...on this rock I will build my church, and the gates of Hades will not overcome it."* (Matthew 16:18)

The church is central to God's plan for redemption in the world. The church is a gift to followers of Jesus—a place of refuge and service and...community. But there is no denying that the function of the church in our culture has shifted dramatically from that of the first local church described in Acts 2. After Jesus has risen from the dead and ascended to Heaven, after the day of Pentecost and the indwelling of the Holy Spirit, we see a beautiful picture of Christian community—the first church.

"They devoted themselves to the apostles' teaching and to fellowship, to the breaking of bread and to prayer. Everyone was filled with awe at the many wonders and signs performed by the apostles. All the believers were together and had everything in common. They sold property and possessions to give to anyone who had need. Every day they continued to meet together in the temple courts. They broke

bread in their homes and ate together with glad and sincere hearts, praising God and enjoying the favor of all the people. And the Lord added to their number daily those who were being saved." (Acts 2:42-47)

This picture of Christian fellowship has been instructive for centuries. Believers gathering in these early days of the church experienced:

- Teaching

- Fellowship

- The sharing of meals

- Prayer

- Commonalities

- Care and commitment to those in need

- Daily meetings

- The praising of God together

- The favor of all the people

- Continual growth in numbers

This passage still serves as the inspiration for church planters and leaders today. It's easy to think, "Wow, doesn't that sound great! Don't we want to have a church like that?" This genuine, committed, passionate community of believers sounds amazing, doesn't it?

We don't doubt that churches and Christian communities like this still exist today—we know they do. However, in our experience, this type of church is very rare in our culture. Instead, the simple, intimate, organic, life-on-life community we see in Acts 2 has been replaced with sprawling church buildings, complex programs, flashy events, and plenty of Sunday-only Christians who aren't very connected to the church outside of the weekend service.

ISOLATION IN COMMUNITY

As Jon Austin writes in the Reformed Journal, much of today's church culture can be attributed to what's known as the "church growth movement."[14] During the 1980s and into the 1990s, churches (pioneered by ministries at Willow Creek Community Church in Chicago and Saddleback Church in Southern California) began to embrace a different way of presenting the church experience.

The church growth strategy is built on very different goals than the traditional goals of community, sacraments, and catechism. It's all about excellence on Sunday mornings—some refer to it as the "Sunday Experience."

Offerings other than Sunday services are typically designed to be relevant and practical, and include experiences as diverse as Trunk or Treat, conferences and symposiums, and Christian concerts.

We don't doubt that the motives and goals of these megachurches and that those involved in the church growth movement are worthy. These churches, leaders, and communities have accomplished some amazing things.

That said, there is no question that this new approach has dramatically changed the way the American church functions. Churches and church leaders across the country (and beyond) began to model their ministry approach after these megachurch success stories. And, as Austin notes, the changes were not all positive:

What effect did this shift in church identity and practice have? As the church growth movement picked up steam, one would expect that church attendance nationally would have begun to move upward. In fact, the opposite occurred.

As the church growth movement increased in influence, church attendance began to decline.

Seeker-sensitive churches—aimed primarily at attracting large audiences—swelled, as smaller, traditional churches shuttered their doors. The fact that congregation members were lost due to this trend is a fact not lost on the pastors of these small churches.

The church growth movement hit its peak around the turn of the century, and yet, as it grew to the pinnacle of its influence, American Christianity witnessed its greatest decline.

There are plenty of reasons for this decline, as we've already seen. But in terms of the effect on the Christian community, a few changes are obvious:

- Many attend church to receive, not to give. In stark contrast to the property-selling and everything-in-common believers in the book of Acts, today we live in a culture far more focused on consuming than participating. In most modern churches people show up, grab a cup of coffee, and enjoy an experience that—for the most part—requires very little audience participation. Oh sure, they might sing along with the songs they recognize, but that's about it.

- Programs are a replacement for community. Let's face it. It is far easier as a church leader to create a program—Bible study, youth group, equipping class, etc.—than it is to develop and promote the concept of a deeply-committed community. As a church member, it's much easier (and far less scary) to attend a once-a-week program than to invite others into your home, or allow people to get to know you on a personal level. Programs are a nice, clean, safe way to have just enough community and participation with the church without being inconvenienced or made uncomfortable.

- People can "easy come, easy go." One of the dark sides of making it easier for people to come to church is that it (usually) makes things easier on the congregants as well. People can slip into church and enjoy services without anyone knowing anything about them—and leave just as easily. There is little commitment required of them unless they take a deliberate step to get more involved.

- Religion has been forever changed by the advent of online church. Just as the Internet has forever changed our culture, so it has shifted the way people interact with the church. Many fast-growing, savvy churches in the church growth movement were among the first to deliver sermons and services, and create personal connections with their members and guests through technology. While we could certainly point out the incredible benefits and opportunities of this technology (Pew Research reported that around 25% of churchgoers in the US utilize online services), there's no doubt that it offers a type of church experience that requires far less in-person interaction.

Again, we're not here to take shots at the modern church, the church growth movement, or online church. There are admirable aspects of massive churches—fine-tuned services and thrilling programs—just as there are also specific strengths in small churches.

God can and does use these things to bring people to the truth of the Gospel. Still, the results of these shifts are clear. Not only are fewer people attending church, but fewer still are experiencing the church as described in the book of Acts—as a genuine, deeply-committed community.

CONNECTING THE DOTS

These shifts in culture, and in the church experience, leave us with some serious holes in community.

The connections we used to enjoy in places like church, school, work, or the marketplace, have been impacted by things like the Internet, online employment, and the increasing mobility—and, thus, relocation—of Americans. The number of Americans living near family members continues to drop yearly.

We can even see these fundamental shifts in something as simple as grocery shopping. According to recent research, grocery delivery services have exploded in popularity with around a quarter of all grocery shoppers ordering online instead of actually going to the store.

All of these things have led to an isolation drift in our daily lives. It's far easier to be alone today than ever before. The only time we really need to leave our homes is to go to the mailbox. And all of this points to the undeniable fact that we need to find new and creative ways to build, extend, and sustain community.

The methods our parents, grandparents, and great-grandparents utilized to connect with others and build community simply aren't as effective, or relevant, today. Bridge clubs are just not a thing anymore, are they? However, I understand that Bunco is making a comeback.

Similarly, the approach our parents and grandparents experienced at church in the past won't necessarily be the answer either. We need to recognize that the deterioration of the church community, and the decline of attendance, won't be reversed if we continue to employ the same strategies over and over.

It's time for a change. We need an approach that recognizes and embraces the major shifts we've experienced in our world and culture. We need to understand how people think, feel, and function.

We've got to get to the heart of the people and the heart of the problem.

However, to fix a problem, we've got to be clear on what's really broken. We need to understand how and where things went wrong. We've spent this chapter discussing American history, but the truth is, we've got to go back a lot further than 2020, or the 1950s, or any time in the history of Western civilization.

To really understand, we have to go back to the very beginning.

CHAPTER 3

HOW THE WORLD GOT SO BROKEN

"Then the Lord God said, 'It is not good that the man should be alone.'"

(Genesis 2:18)

STORIES FROM THE FRONT

Jeff: Ross and Kylie, along with their two young children, moved from Texas to Colorado in 2018. They settled into what seemed like the perfect neighborhood for a young family. And for a while, it was.

The neighborhood kids spent their days outside. The adults were open and friendly. Neighborhood picnics and BBQs were commonplace.

But then came 2020, and everything changed.

No one saw the COVID pandemic coming. While each of us reacted differently, there was one thing we all had in common. The realization that life as we knew it was gone.

Ross and Kylie began noticing their neighbors pulling away and isolating. Gone were the outdoor play parties. Gone were the BBQs. Neighbors were now far more likely to pull into their driveways and hunker down behind closed doors.

Distancing became even worse during the 2020 presidential race. As "Trump" and "Biden" signs were firmly planted in front yards throughout the neighborhood, the air became thick with feelings of competition and even contempt. Suddenly, a neighborhood built on community and openness became a pit of isolation and disagreement.

After the election was called in November of 2020, the family's block became even more severed as the 50% whose candidate won and the 50% whose candidate lost, partied and pouted, respectively.

How did this happen? How, in just one year, did an entire neighborhood change so drastically due to a pandemic and politics?

More importantly, how is it possible to recapture the sweetness and simplicity of this community?

FALLING APART

We've gained significant insight by looking at the changes that have taken place over recent decades in our churches and our culture.

However, the truth is that the most central challenge to community isn't new. In reality, barriers to connecting with others have been present since the beginning—literally, the very beginning of the world.

In Genesis, the first book of the Bible, a beautiful picture of God's perfect creation is conveyed. He has made real the sun, moon, and stars, the birds of the air and fish of the sea, the land and the water.

God calls his creation "good." Everything is the way it should be. But then something interesting happens in the creation account.

"Then God said, 'Let us make man in our image, after our likeness. And let them have dominion over the fish of the sea and over the birds of the heavens and over the livestock and over all the earth and over every creeping thing that creeps on the earth.'" **(Genesis 1:26)**

There's a profound truth in these verses. Notice that God says, "Let us make man in our image." Who is the "us" He is talking about here?

This verse is what theologians point to as one of the first presentations of the Trinity—that God exists as three persons in one: the Father, the Son (Jesus) and the Holy Spirit.

Here, at the very beginning of creation, we see that God exists in community. God the Father, Jesus the Son, and the Holy Spirit are working together in creation.

They create two creatures—man and woman—a reflection of their collective image.

"So God created man in his own image, in the image of God He created him; male and female He created them." **(Genesis 1:27)**

In Genesis 2 we are presented more information about the origins of humankind. We become privy to God's thought process in designing both man and woman. Adam is created first, but when God observes Adam's lonely existence, he makes an interesting statement:

"Then the Lord God said, 'It is not good that the man should be alone; I will make him a helper fit for him.'" **(Genesis 2:18)**

Following the conception and realization of Earth and man, and setting in motion the rhythm of the universe, we see, for the first time, God questioning his creation, referring to it as "not good." Something is wrong with this picture. Adam, alone in Paradise, does not reflect God's character or creative design.

So God makes a partner for Adam, a "helper fit for him," also in his image. God, who exists in community realized that Adam needed Eve, and Eve needed Adam.

Human beings need each other. It's in our DNA.

From the very beginning, we were made for community. And here's the incredible thing: The community that Adam and Eve experienced was perfect.

In fact, Genesis 2 says, *"the man and his wife were both naked and were not ashamed."* There is no reason for them to be ashamed. They are made for each other. They are husband and wife, made into one flesh.

"Then the man said, 'This at last is bone of my bones and flesh of my flesh; she shall be called Woman, because she was taken out of Man. Therefore a man shall leave his father and his mother and hold fast to his wife, and they shall become one flesh. And the man and his wife were both naked and were not ashamed.'" **(Genesis 2:23-24)**

In the Garden, we see a picture of perfect community between two people: an intimate relationship with no fear, shame, or separation. Adam and Eve experience this kind of genuine community with each other—and with God. They share everything and enjoy everything together. There is no conflict or communication barrier.

But a chapter later in the Biblical account, everything changes. In Genesis 3, a new character is introduced to this picture-perfect story—the serpent. This slithery deceiver (more crafty than any other beast of the field that the Lord God had made) asks a simple question of Eve. *"Did God actually say, 'You shall not eat of any tree in the Garden?'"* (Genesis 3:1-2)

Eve remembers God's command: You may eat from any tree in the Garden but one, which will surely cause death.

But the crafty snake presses further, saying to Eve, *"You will not surely die. For God knows that when you eat of it your eyes will be opened, and you will be like God, knowing good and evil."* (Genesis 3:4-5)

You could boil down the intention of the serpent (who we know from the rest of Scripture is Satan himself) to one simple strategy—create a chasm between Eve and God. He accomplishes this by sowing within Eve seeds of distrust in her Creator.

"Did God actually say that?"

"Can you really trust his word?"

"Maybe he's holding out on you."

As you read Genesis 3, you can almost feel the tension in Eve's heart (and, of course, in her husband Adam's as well). Suddenly, doubt in God and his great design rears its ugly head.

Adam and Eve begin to question their identity and purpose in this idyllic setting. They wonder who this God really is and whether he can really be trusted. In this moment, the serpent makes his move. Sadly, Adam and Eve take the bait.

"So when the woman saw that the tree was good for food and that it was a delight to the eyes, and that the tree was to be desired to make one wise, she took of its fruit and ate,

and she also gave some to her husband who was with her, and he ate." **(Genesis 3:6)**

The rest of the story reads like a tragedy. Adam and Eve have a sudden realization that they are naked (that thought hadn't crossed their minds before). Their instincts inform them to hide from each other—and from God.

But, God, of course, knows where to find them. And, when he does, he pronounces judgment on them—and on the serpent. Adam and Eve are then cast out of the Garden. It may be difficult to understand, but these consequences are blessed with God's grace.

For, if Adam and Eve remain in the garden, they will live eternally without a relationship with God. Instead, God puts an expiration date on human life. And so begins the story of the Bible—one that, gratefully, does not end there.

There is so much to learn from this story. It's as relevant today as it was in the beginning. It's the basis for the way we think about community, relationships, and the origin of the conflicts we face. The reality is that our relationships with each other—spouses, families, friends, coworkers, and yes, neighbors—have all been influenced by the results of the fall in Genesis 3.

Here are some key takeaways from the Genesis account:

Takeaway #1

There is a palpable force that seeks to disconnect us from God and each other.

In scripture, the identity of that force is made very clear. It is the Serpent—the Devil—the enemy of God and his people.

We're guessing you haven't seen a crafty serpent slithering around in your house lately. However, you probably can relate to the idea that it feels like something—or someone— is pulling you away from those you most want and need to relate to, including God himself.

If you are a person of faith, you can likely relate to the feeling that so much of our world, our lives, and our hearts can draw us away from a deeper and more connected relationship with God. Just ask any Christian how their daily abiding in Jesus is going, or how often they make time to quietly read the Bible and pray. You're likely to get some serious hemming and hawing.

Why is that? It's because we live in a world that is full of distractions and obstacles to a deep spiritual life. These include work, noise, entertainment, money, temptations, conflict, cable news, mortgages, and dentist appointments (apologies to all dentists reading this, we are grateful for you... really). All of these demands in our lives pull us in a million directions, often leading us away from God, and from those we know we need the most.

And if we're not careful, even good and necessary things in our lives can pull us away from people as well. Just as we often feel the tension of not having enough time to spend with the Word or in prayer, we can also identify with the feeling that we don't have enough quality time with people. Our spouses. Our kids. Our friends. Let alone our neighbors.

It seems like the world almost wants us to be anywhere other than where we are. At work, we worry about home life. At home, we think about work. During a busy week, we dream of a vacation. On vacation, we can't stop feeling anxious about how full our email inbox is becoming. On and on and on it goes.

There are lots of practical thoughts on how we can address these challenges. For a moment, though, let's just consider that perhaps the same force that drove Adam and Eve to eat from the forbidden tree in Genesis 3 still exists today. Maybe there is still a crafty enemy who wants to constantly pull us away from God and from each other.

The Bible backs up this idea. In the New Testament, Paul says, *"We do not wrestle against flesh and blood, but against the rulers, against the authorities, against the cosmic powers over this present darkness, against the spiritual forces of evil in the heavenly places."* (Ephesians 6:12). This verse comes on the heels of Paul's writing about (guess what?) relationships. Workers and masters. Wives and husbands. Children and parents. The Church.

It would be naive for us to think that our enemy isn't still out to drive a wedge between us and God, and between us and the people he has placed in our lives. It's kind of his thing.

There is an enemy who wants to isolate us from our communities. And he's pretty good at doing it.

It makes sense, right? The success of Satan's approach in the Garden still works effectively today. The more people are pulled away from healthy and loving relationships, the more they struggle. The more people struggle, the more they feel a need to hide their brokenness. The more they live in isolation, the harder it is to heal.

Takeaway #2

Sin results in broken relationships. As we've seen, not only do the events of Genesis 3 affect our relationship with God, but they also mess with our personal relationships.

This is evident in the Garden story as well. What's the first thing Adam does when God asks him about eating the fruit? He blames his wife!

"He said, 'Who told you that you were naked? Have you eaten of the tree of which I commanded you not to eat?' The man said, 'The woman whom you gave to be with me, she gave me fruit of the tree, and I ate.'" (Genesis 3:11-12)

Think about that for a moment. God has given Adam an incredible gift—a woman to be his helper and mate, built from his very rib. This is flesh of Adam's flesh, bone of his bones.

Yet, after the decision to sin, the first defense he thinks of is, "It's her fault!" And, in his plan B, he blames his Creator. "God, it's your fault. You created her for me!"

And just like that, marital conflict enters the world. We know this conflict isn't limited only to marital relationships, but it infiltrates every single human interaction.

This tragic story continues throughout Scripture, particularly in the Old Testament, where we see mankind experience struggles with one another in every way possible—through violence, jealousy, anger, deceit, assault, theft...you name it. It isn't pretty.

Things get so ugly with mankind that Genesis says: *"The Lord saw that the wickedness of man was great in the earth, and that every intention of the thoughts of his heart was only evil continually."* (Genesis 6:5)

So, what does this have to do with us today? Well, for one thing, it should help explain why the world can seem so ugly and hopeless at times.

On a more personal level, it explains why we feel so much distance from one another in our human experience. Our natural state is to deeply desire human connection, like what God designed for Adam and Eve in the Garden. Yet everything in our experience and our flesh tempts us to run away from—or fight against—one other.

Put two human beings in an otherwise indifferent environment, and it won't take long for conflict to arise. Don't believe it? Just watch a couple of toddlers in a playroom for a few minutes.

Conflict brews because we want things our way instead of the way God intended. This is what the Bible calls sin— choosing our own path instead of God's.

Our sinful nature is to place our needs and desires over anyone else's. This leads us to an unhealthy view of ourselves and others.

In that fateful moment in the Garden, when Adam's sin is exposed before God, he treats Eve not as his wife, but as his enemy! He—for a moment at least—hopes God will punish her and get him off the hook.

If we're honest, this isn't so different from what we do any time we sin against the people in our own lives. We choose to ignore our spouse's needs so we can meet our own. (Do you take the bigger bowl of ice cream?) We prioritize our comfort over serving our family. We are dishonest with a friend to avoid negative consequences. We put on a facade to avoid the risk of rejection or judgment.

Sin is a grenade of selfishness thrown into the heart of any relationship. The effects are always destructive.

Now, inject into this reality the modern toxicity of social media, politics, class tensions, money, etc., and you have the recipe for an explosion. It's a bit like handing those two toddlers a single chocolate chip cookie and telling them to decide who gets to eat it. It's not going to end well!

We have to find a way to deal with the sin that separates us, or we will continue to run fast and far away from the people with whom we were meant to be connected. It's in our fallen DNA.

Takeaway #3

Because of our brokenness, we tend to hide, and we experience an emotion that adds even further to the separation we feel from one another.

That feeling is shame.

Shame is a deep sense that we will be judged, disciplined, or even cut off because of our bad actions and characteristics.

It is shame that leads to isolation in the Garden for Adam and Eve. God's response after their moral failure was a question: "Where are you, Adam?"

Adam and Eve were hiding. Why? Because they were ashamed and afraid.

"But the Lord God called to the man and said to him, 'Where are you?' And he said, 'I heard the sound of you in the garden, and I was afraid, because I was naked, and I hid myself.' He said, 'Who told you that you were naked? Have you eaten of the tree of which I commanded you not to eat?'" **(Genesis 3:9-11)**

It's a heartbreaking scene, these two people hiding from the very one who created and loved them. The only one who could heal their wounds and make them whole again.

Shame is something our culture rarely talks about, but it is still rampant in our souls today. It is driving us apart.

As researcher Brené Brown explains it, *"Shame is basically the fear of being unlovable. Shame is the feeling you get when you believe that you're not worthy of anyone caring about you or loving you. That you're such a bad person that you can't even blame other people for not caring about you."*[15]

When we feel ashamed, we feel as though we have to pull away from others. Why? Because if it's true that we're unlovable, bad people, then being around others can be incredibly scary—and even considered dangerous.

What is riskier for a flawed person (every one of us) than being really known by others?

What's more terrifying than knocking on your neighbors' door when you've lived next to them for years but don't even know their names? What's harder than taking a step toward someone without having any idea how they'll respond to you? What's trickier than rebuilding a relationship that suffered a rocky period?

Many of us have felt the sting of rejection many times from friends and family. That rejection has left us with a deep feeling of shame. It can be easy to think, "Something is wrong with me; that's why I was rejected. I wasn't good enough or strong enough or pretty enough or whatever enough for that person. And I won't ever be."

With shame dragging alongside us through life, the last thing we want to do is put our hearts and souls on the line to get to know our neighbors.

To make matters worse, we perceive a desire for isolation from others as well. So when our neighbor drives straight into their garage and closes the door rather than risk an interaction with us as we stand in our front yard, we get the message, "I'm not interested in being known; please stay away." If we're honest, maybe a part of us is relieved to receive that message. It lets us off the hook. No obligation required.

In many ways, we are still a lot like Adam and Eve in the Garden. We are afraid, hiding with our shame, and missing something deep and good and restorative. We are left lacking the God-given gift of community.

CHAPTER 4

PARTY FOUL: LIFE WITHOUT COMMUNITY

"One of the tragedies of our life is...
we keep forgetting who we are."
—Henri Nouwen

STORIES FROM THE FRONT

Jeff: Our friends, John and Kristen, recently moved to a new neighborhood with their young kids. As they got to know their neighbors, they realized there was one unique challenge on the block—and she happened to be right next door.

This woman had lived in her home for many years and was known as the black sheep of the neighborhood. Her house was run down, her grass rarely trimmed, her yard a mess. Her dogs could be heard barking at all hours of the night. And the police made more than one visit to her home.

Because of this, most of the neighbors were frustrated with her. She was seen as a nuisance, a bother, and her home detracted from an otherwise nice, well-kept street. They made a point of avoiding her.

At first, it was easy for John and Kristen to feel the same way. But as time went on, they found themselves prompted to reach out to her in some way.

One snowy morning, an opportunity presented itself. John decided to shovel the foot or so of snow from her driveway and sidewalk. Afterward, Kristen dropped off a loaf of freshly-baked bread.

Those good deeds did not go unnoticed. Their neighbor was incredibly grateful—even stunned at their kindness. She reached out to express her thanks and how much it meant to her.

In the weeks to follow, John and Kristen learned more about her life. One of the stories she shared was about her family. Several years earlier, in a tragic accident, she lost her husband as he was saving one of their children from drowning.

Suddenly, the bigger picture came into view. This woman wasn't a problem, she was a precious person with a heartbreaking story of pain and loss. Hearing her story changed John and Kristen's perspective of her entirely.

Yes, the dogs still bark. And no, the grass still isn't always cut. This woman may never be their best friend. But she is their neighbor. And John and Kristen are committed to treating her as one.

THE COST OF LONELINESS

Picture yourself arriving home from work, school, or running an errand. As you drive/walk/scooter back into the neighborhood, what do you see around you? More than likely, you see a diverse group of people—different ages, backgrounds, lifestyles, and maybe different cultures.

But do you see community? Do you see people who are connected to each other in real and meaningful ways? Or, as is true for many, do you see a whole lot of people operating in their own little bubbles, rarely interacting with one another except for the occasional wave hello?

Are you one of those people? It would be easy to think this is normal. And truthfully, we're never going to be close to every person we know. But if we choose not to interact with, and get to know, those living around us, we need to be aware of the cost.

The cost is loneliness. You may be experiencing that loneliness right now—a feeling that you don't really know the people around you, and that they don't really know you. Perhaps you've experienced too many evening walks and Saturday breakfasts alone. Or maybe loneliness isn't your current experience. But if the statistics are correct (and we believe they are) it is likely that someone on your street is certainly experiencing it.

And here's the thing. Loneliness doesn't just make us sad. It's not simply an emotion. It becomes part of our identity, like a cancerous cell that multiplies inside of us, robbing us of the things that are most important to our identity. Ultimately, the true cost of loneliness is experiencing the loss of who we were made to be. When we aren't connected with others in deep, meaningful relationships, our sense of self begins to break down in significant ways.

OUR SENSE OF VALUE

Since we were designed to live in community, the absence of it can corrode our sense of worth. When we work and live with others, we are blessed with the opportunity to serve, love, care for, forgive, and support in a way that is incredibly meaningful and long-lasting.

OUR SENSE OF SECURITY

If you've ever traveled abroad, you probably understand that feeling of uneasiness that can set in when you are in an unknown place, surrounded by unknown people speaking a language you don't understand. It is this fear of the unknown that keeps many from traveling.

But what a shame it is when this feeling permeates our own neighborhoods. If we feel surrounded by strangers and the unknown, we're bound to feel unsafe, unwelcome, and exposed to some degree.

And if we feel that way, chances are our neighbors do, too. Do your neighbors feel safe and secure living next to you?

OUR SENSE OF OPTIMISM

When you look at your neighbors, what do you find yourself thinking? "These are great people! They have flaws for sure, but what great potential they all have to contribute to, and grow in, community!"

Or, are you more likely thinking, "These people are so weird, so different, so untrustworthy, I can't believe people like this exist in my world! If the lens through which we see our neighbors is always one of negativity, community becomes impossible.

Is there anything more discouraging than believing the world is only getting worse? Christian theology supports this idea to some extent: We know we live in a broken world that won't be made right until Jesus returns.

Remember the last book of the Bible? For those whose faith is in Jesus, we're headed for a massive party. And at that party, God will make all things new. We will live in a perfect relationship with him and each other. Is there a better reason for optimism?

OUR SENSE OF JOY

It is certainly possible to experience joy by ourselves. Ask any introvert, and they will tell you there is a unique joy in being alone.

However, if people (yes, even you, introverts) remain alone for too long, they will likely sense something eating away at their soul.

We long for connection, community, and belonging. And we have an innate desire to matter to someone else. So when we experience these feelings, it produces an unmistakable joy.

Consider this: What image comes to mind when you think of someone experiencing true joy?

- A parent at the birth of their child?

- A couple celebrating their wedding day?

- A crowd cheering their favorite team's big win?

- A child playing with their friends or family?

- A group of friends on an epic road trip together?

What is the common thread running through all these joyful occasions? They are experienced with other human beings. There is no escaping that our greatest joys are experienced together.

Science backs this up. Studies have shown that the most sustainable joy is joy that is shared.[16] As German Nobel Peace Prize winner Albert Schweitzer said, *"Happiness is the only thing that multiplies when you share it."*

In fact, research also shows that smiling, or even seeing someone smile, releases dopamine, serotonin, and endorphins that make us feel happier. Spreading joy isn't just a good thing to do, it's good for our health. Science backs it up.

THE TWO-SIDED COIN

This brings us to a complication. After all, there is a not-so-pretty side to the Highland cow. (Hey, didn't we say the party's in the front?) Just as our joy, optimism, and sense of value are intertwined with our relationships, so, too—on the not-so-pretty side—are our pain, hurt, and sorrows.

It is true that, at times, life seems like it would be easier without other people. Still, it would certainly be very lonely, wouldn't it? Remember the Genesis story? Adam was in paradise, experiencing a perfect relationship with God, and yet there was something about Adam's aloneness that God found to be "not good."

And yet, when God gives to Adam the incredible gift of Eve, the stage is set for potential disaster. Ultimately, Adam chooses his wife over obedience to God. He doesn't step in to stop her from eating the forbidden fruit, and ultimately follows her in choosing the same sin.

As we've seen, the result of this sin is brokenness in all human relationships. This is the tragedy of the incredibly important Bible story that kicks off in Genesis 3.

Simply put, community is like a double-sided coin. On the one hand, our relationships with others can be one of the greatest sources of joy in our lives. On the other, these same relationships can sometimes be fraught with pain, feelings of rejection, and suffering.

This is where our perspective on community becomes so important. Understanding where things became so broken helps us to make sense of the many wrongs in our culture and communities today.

In tracing the roots of our interpersonal problems back to the beginning of Genesis, we begin to understand the cause and effect of loneliness, the gift of interconnection, and when—and why—our relationship with God, and our relationships with each other, began to fall apart.

In the Garden, Adam and Eve fell as a result of the very things that made them human. They fell despite being blessed with God-given community.

It's through this filter that we are able to observe, and begin to understand, some of the biggest challenges we face in our world today, and how to view them in a new light.

These "party fouls," as we'll call them have been precursors to some of the most blatant, relevant, and explosive issues to ever ravage our communities, preventing us from immersing ourselves in the life and love that God designed us to experience with others.

Here are just a few...

Party Foul #1: Political Division

Perhaps one of the biggest sources of division in our culture today is politics. Yes, it seems some the dirtiest words you can utter these days are "conservative," "liberal," "Republican," and "Democrat," depending upon the person with whom you're speaking. Introduce CNN and Fox News to the conversation and get ready for the fireworks. If you really want to throw some dynamite on a great party, start talking politics.

In American culture, government and politics have always been sources of contention and dissension—a reality set into motion when the founding fathers drew up the Constitution and created a representative government to be elected of the people, by the people, and for the people.

Democracy is a good thing in many, many ways, but it sure is messy. It means that there will always be tension between groups with differing perspectives and opposing political party affiliations in our country. There always has been. (Remember the Civil War?)

Still, modern-day political division does seem to be of a new, more intense flavor than in past eras. Let's look at some numbers.

According to Pew Research, 40% of Democrats today say they are consistently liberal in their views, versus just 8% back in 1994. The numbers are similar on the opposing side, as 33% of Republicans report being consistently conservative versus just 10% a decade ago. In other words, more and more of us have developed unwavering and inflexible views on political issues.

In a 2020 study, Pew Research found that 39% of Donald Trump supporters had no friends who supported the opposing party's candidate. Meanwhile, 42% of Joe Biden supporters said they had no friends who supported Trump. Only 3% of Trump and Biden supporters said they had a lot of friends who supported the other side.[16]

We're not here to debate politics (so go ahead and breathe a deep sigh of relief). However, we do think it's important to realize (if you haven't already) that our country is becoming more and more extreme in its political views.

This trend cannot be separated from our larger discussion on community. When people are less and less connected to each other, they tend to believe fewer positive things about others. When people find community only in echo chambers on social media, the walls between them and others only grow higher and stronger. In such a scenario, it doesn't take much to light a match that can set conflict ablaze in relationships, communities, and countries.

As Robert D. Putnam writes in *Bowling Alone*, *"People divorced from community, occupation, and association are first and foremost among the supporters of extremism."*[17]

In other words, the more divided we become on political issues, the more likely we are to retreat to hardline positions and actions. If I don't know anyone who is a member of the opposing party, or who sees the world differently, it becomes easier to demonize them, to inflate their negatives, and to regard them as the enemy.

Remember when the breakdown began in the Garden? There was, and still is, a real enemy who wants to drive us away from God and each other. When we choose our own way (sin) instead of God's, our relationships begin to suffer. As a result, our desire to pull away from each other increases in intensity.

The results of this choice can be seen in today's political climate as much as anywhere else. Whose agenda are we living for? The agenda of our preferred political party? Or, perhaps, that of our favorite candidate?

Instead, we are called to live out God's agenda for our lives. Jesus reminds us that our agendas should be aligned with those of God's Kingdom. Our desire should be to experience his teachings in practice on this Earth. And a massive step in that direction is learning to forgive others, as we are forgiven by God through Jesus.

Here's what Jesus tells his disciples to pray in The Lord's Prayer.

"Our Father in heaven, hallowed be your name. Your kingdom come, your will be done, on Earth as it is in heaven. Give us this day our daily bread, and forgive us our debts, as we also have forgiven our debtors. And lead us not into temptation, but deliver us from evil." **(Matthew 6:9-13)**

Living our lives with this perspective as our guiding light brings us closer to one another, and to God. And striving to live a life worthy of entering the Eternal Kingdom quickly puts our earthly kingdom in proper perspective.

Party Foul #2: The Racial Divide

The cultural divide in our country certainly isn't limited to politics. In fact, it seems like a perfect storm when it comes to the cultural challenges that face us in the United States.

While the racial divide feels like less of a present reality for many of us in our given contexts, there is no denying that racial tension in our culture has been on the rise in recent years. Research found that 58% of Americans believe race relations in this country to be bad—and the vast majority of citizens believe it's only getting worse.[18]

Whatever we believe to be the cause for this, we simply can't deny it's a problem that creates serious cracks in the core of community.

Today, many of our neighborhoods, schools, and cultural centers remain racially segregated to some degree, even though segregation ended legally decades ago.

Unfortunately, racial divisions also exist within the American church. The Pew Religion in Public Life survey found that 75% of white evangelicals said they attend churches that are mostly white, and roughly the same amount (74%) of black protestants said they are a part of mostly black congregations.[19]

We could debate the reasons for this for a long time (and it's a worthy discussion), but there's no denying that the American church is far from unified along racial lines.

What is that different picture supposed to look like? Well, simply put, there should be no racial or ethnic divisions within the church. Neither should there be disunity based on race, gender, class, or politics. Regardless of differences, anyone in search of a personal relationship with Jesus Christ should be welcomed.

This is exactly what Paul writes about in Ephesians. His letter to the church in Ephesus is a plea to both Jews (God's chosen nation throughout history up to that point) and Gentiles (pretty much everybody else) to now live as one unified people in Christ.

When we read the words in Ephesians 2 today, we may think, "Oh yeah, that makes sense. Jews and Gentiles should be united in their religious pursuits. Got it!"

However, we overlook the mind-bending, earth-shattering reality shift this would have been for both Jews and the Gentiles at the time Paul wrote these words. These two groups weren't only different in every conceivable way, they were sworn enemies. They were diametrically opposed to each other in their religious, traditional, cultural, political, and, yes, racial ideals.

The Jews, of course, had a significant place in history as God's chosen people. They lived differently and believed differently than the cultures with whom they shared physical spaces. Over time, their identity as God's chosen people became twisted. In many ways, they began to see themselves as superior to other people. A combination of the fear of contamination and pride in the Jewish mind created a prejudicial disdain for—even revulsion toward— what they considered to be the idolatrous and unclean Gentiles.

On the other side, the Gentiles truly disliked and distrusted the Jewish people. They thought Jewish religious practices were bizarre, and resented the way they carried themselves.

In short, there were huge philosophical and theological divides. But, there was a literal divide—in the temple in Jerusalem—to prevent Gentiles from passing too far into the house of worship. Only Jews could pass that wall. Trespassing was punishable by death.

So when Paul writes these words in Ephesians, it is completely revolutionary. Here's what he says:

"Therefore remember that at one time you Gentiles in the flesh, called 'the uncircumcision' by what is called the circumcision, which is made in the flesh by hands—remember that you were at that time separated from Christ, alienated from the commonwealth of Israel and strangers to the covenants of promise, having no hope and without God in the world. But now in Christ Jesus you who once were far off have been brought near by the blood of Christ. For he himself is our peace, who has made us both one and has broken down in his flesh the dividing wall of hostility." **(Ephesians 2:11-14)**

Paul, a Jew himself, tells the Ephesian Christians that the wall separating their two cultures has been destroyed. They are now called to be one people because of what Jesus has accomplished through his death and resurrection.

What this meant was that these groups of people that had so little in common now shared something greater than anything else—faith in Jesus. They were now united by Christ's sacrifice on the cross. This reality enabled they could live differently, and live together.

We don't know everything about the early days of the church in Ephesus, but what we can glean from Paul's letter is that the reality of togetherness wasn't pretty and, in fact, was a daily struggle for Jews and Gentiles. Any time you attempt to bring together people from different backgrounds, different cultures, and different traditions, there is going to be—at the very least—awkwardness and misunderstanding. And at worst, serious conflict.

In Jesus, the church now had an opportunity to present a very different picture to the world around it. Imagine what this looked like to that culture! The city of Ephesus now saw Jewish and Gentile Christians ending their conflict with, and disdain for, one another. They were now actually...loving each other? Living life together? Sharing meals?

How could this be?

There was only one explanation. Something radical had happened to these people: a complete identity transformation that altered the way they saw themselves and each other.

Such transformations still exist for today's church. The impact of Christ's death and resurrection is no less powerful and life-changing today than it was at the time of Paul's writings in Ephesians.

However, if people observe followers of Jesus living in the same cultural boxes, what's going to convince them that they—and their differing perspectives and lifestyles—would be genuinely welcomed into the Christian community?

STORIES FROM THE FRONT

Jeff: Today, the idea of moving somewhere less comfortable than where you currently live is incredibly rare, if not downright unheard of.

Still, that's exactly what Jason and Wendy's family did in 2023. For years, they longed to live in an ethnically and demographically diverse community with a church in which that diversity was being lived out intentionally.

So, after many conversations, hours of research, and countless prayers, they decided to move their family to a very diverse suburb of Denver, Colorado. Here, they would be surrounded by significant populations of more than thirty ethnicities including blacks, whites, Ethiopians, East Indians, Burmese, and Mexicans.

Their church is on a mission to live out the Biblical vision of oneness we see in Scripture. It is composed of two

---

> previous congregations—one predominantly white and the other predominantly black—who have come together to worship and live for Jesus.
>
> That's exactly what Jason and Wendy had been searching for.

Party Foul #3: Busyness

Okay, so we've looked at the effect politics and racial tension have on our sense of community. Now, we're on to the obvious next obstacle—busyness.

Wait...what? Yep. Busyness is another major party foul when it comes to community and connection in our culture today.

Think about it. What are some of the most common reasons you cite for not connecting with others—whether it's your family, friends, coworkers, fellow church members, or neighbors? It's not often for some big, dramatic reason. Excuses like "I just can't seem to find the time" and "life is so crazy lately" are far more commonplace.

We are smack in the middle of an overly-busy school/sports/work decades-long season. It'll lighten up soon, right? (Spoiler alert: It may lighten up from time to time but it will never vanish.)

Maybe it's our assumption about the busyness of others and the fear of being a burden on the already-burned-out people in your life that prevents us from reaching out. After all, if your neighbors feel as busy as you do, you certainly don't want to put any more pressure on them.

As a society, we are busier today than ever before. In 2017, a Pew Research study found that 60% of American adults felt they were at least sometimes too busy to enjoy life.

For parents, that number was even higher, with 74% of those with kids making this "too-busy" claim. And the percentage of parents who said they were too busy to read to their children at night was 75%![20] (As parents of young children ourselves, even we can report that—at this very moment—we could both really use a nap).

It makes sense, right? We live in a world that is so fast-paced and so technologically driven that the things we try to accomplish in an average day are way more ambitious than ever.

If you feel like your to-do list is never-ending, you're not alone. Benjamin Franklin is credited with developing an early form of the to-do list. His daily question to himself was, *"What good have I done today?"*

Centuries later, our to-do lists are much more complicated, and include many, if not all of the following (or more):

- Pay that bill, and that one, and later, that one

- Check emails

- Check texts

- Pay more bills

- Call that person back

- Respond (finally) to the person who texted you four days ago

- Check the news

- Get the oil changed on the car

- Run errands

- Pick up the kids from (name any of the million possible activities)

- Clean the house

- Make house repairs

- Check your emails again

- Pay more bills

- How is it possible that I have 18 unread text messages already?

We know you can relate. This sort of never-ending to-do list, and constant phone, email and text reminders can be extremely draining, distracting, and frustrating.

Here's what reporter Joe Pinsker wrote in an article for *The Atlantic* titled, *Ugh, I'm so Busy: A Status Symbol for Our Time.*

"The mundane yet fraught place where these various obligations converge is the to-do list. Americans have long felt that they had too much to do, but in the past few decades, this feeling seems to have become more common and intense, as new breeds of tasks have emerged and people's finite mental energies have been depleted by changes to the modern economy. For many, the to-do list, whether written or mental, now suffers from a sort of infinite scroll: Reaching the end of it can be unimaginable."[21]

The infinite scroll. A great band name. A terrible reality.

So, whether we actually have all that much to do or not, it certainly seems like we do. That simple fact can make us feel too busy or too exhausted (or both) to reach out to people around us. We are already responsible for so many relationships in our lives (family, friends, coworkers, etc.). Where, and how, in the world are we supposed to fit all these things in?

The result is that we often miss connecting with the people who live steps away from our front door.

TO SUM IT ALL UP

Okay, take a deep breath with us. It can feel incredibly discouraging to dwell on the many ways in which we see brokenness in our world's relationships and community. Maybe you disagree with some of our interpretations of the culture and the church (It's okay. We aren't going to yell at you. That's hard to do through a book, anyway.)

Here's the bottom line: We have to recognize what's wrong in order to fix it.

And while it's overwhelming, it can also be incredibly freeing for us to realize that the problems we face in our modern culture aren't at all new. They've been a part of the story of humanity since Genesis.

Discovering the roots of these challenges helps us understand how things became so broken in the first place. We can't simply blame one thing— a person, a political party, a philosophy, an event in time, or even ourselves. Though all of these things play a part, they aren't the true reason behind our struggles to create community.

The true reason lies in the very fabric of mankind. What became broken in the Garden between humans and God, and between humans and each other, remains broken today. And the results are all around us. These are the party fouls that trip us up in our pursuit of community.

But a party foul doesn't have to ruin a great party. There is still hope—a ton.

Why? Because the story of Scripture doesn't end in the Garden—that's just the beginning of God's plan unfolding. In fact, this story offers us the exact blueprint we need to overcome this brokenness, restore relationships, and create a community that brings us closer to God and to each other.

There is a way to mend that brokenness—to reconnect to the light despite the darkness and despair of our broken world. There is a way back to a place full of joy, laughter, music, and community.

Ahh, can you hear it? The sounds of a party are beginning to stir.

CHAPTER 5

THE WAY BACK

"The Gospel is this: We are more sinful and flawed in ourselves than we ever dared believe, yet at the very same time, we are more loved and accepted in Jesus Christ than we ever dared hope." —Tim Keller

---

STORIES FROM THE FRONT

Jeff: When we moved into our neighborhood several years ago, we quickly discovered that we had a unique opportunity to meet our new neighbors.

Our house sits on an apron—a small, separate drive between our house and the main street in our neighborhood.

This design presented to us a new (and surprising) reality: We were now spending most of our time in our front yard. Our four girls love being on their bikes, making chalk art, climbing trees, and building forts.

And they do all these things (and dozens more) in full view of everyone who comes by.

As you can imagine, four little girls playing, creating, and making joyful messes in the front yard became quite the bright spot in our neighborhood. And because our street sits at the main entrance to the neighborhood, just about everyone soon knew who we were.

Now, almost every time we're outside, we interact with at least one of our neighbors. Or neighbors will stop to say "hi" and see what the girls are up to as they are driving by. The Amazon and UPS drivers know our names (and hone their driving skills by dodging balls, dolls, and scooters strewn about our drive).

To be honest, this reality was a bit overwhelming at first. At times since, I've thought to myself how much quieter life would be if we spent more time in the backyard, and were not constantly on display to the world.

However, my wife and I—and our kids—have come to appreciate this reality. We've gotten to know so many of our neighbors. Our kids have brought smiles to so many faces. We've heard stories of joy and pain. We've had neighbors join soccer games and make suggestions about the girls' daily front yard projects. We've even had the opportunity to pray with our neighbors.

And all of this came from simply being available—and being willing to be seen and known, and making an effort to get to know others. It's not always easy, but it's always positive.

There truly is a party in the front at the Dillon home on a very regular basis, and we wouldn't have it any other way.

AN INNER TRANSFORMATION

There's a saying my wife and I return to when thinking about addressing a problem: "It wasn't broken overnight, so it won't be fixed overnight."

If the reasons for our lack of connection in community are internal, and deeply rooted in our humanity, then it makes sense that the road toward genuine community won't be a quick or easy one.

After all, we aren't going to instantly feel safe opening up to others just because we think we should. In fact, the feeling that we ought to be more connected with people can often cause guilt, which just leads us to more disconnection!

Neither can we expect people to immediately begin opening up their lives to us just because we offer them a cup of coffee.

The truth is, getting to know your neighbors can be tough. And the challenges we face are both great, and deeply ingrained in who we are as people.

So how do we deal with all these obstacles to connection? How do we become known? How do we find our way back to truly knowing others? How do we create neighborhoods and friend groups and churches that are open, welcoming, and full of gracious love for each other?

Is it even possible? We believe it is. But here's the catch—the biggest change that's needed in your neighborhood doesn't begin with a knock on the door or a fun event (we'll get to those soon). It begins with you.

You see, the road to genuine community and connection with others starts not with something outside of us, but with something within us. We need to recognize the long-held attitudes and emotions that keep us from moving toward people. And as we begin to make that move, we need to be in a place to accept the awkwardness and hurt that can ensue as a result.

If we expect people to come to a party, we have to be convinced ourselves that the party is worth attending! This means that we may need an inner transformation, one that reshapes the way we see ourselves and those around us.

This is the power of the Gospel.

THE GOSPEL

What is the Gospel? Put simply, it is the good news that God sent his son, Jesus, to live a perfect life on our behalf, to die on a cross and pay the penalty for our sins, and to rise again so that we might have life in and through him.

The Bible tells us that the only way to Heaven is by God's grace, through faith in Jesus. *"Jesus said to him, 'I am the way, and the truth, and the life. No one comes to the Father except through me.'"* (John 14:6)

When we repent of our sins and trust in Jesus as our Lord and Savior, our sins are forgiven, and God declares us righteous—made whole in the sight of our Holy Creator. And this means we will experience life everlasting in Heaven.

This is the best news the world has ever known, and it is a message anyone can embrace by simply renouncing their way and, instead, trusting in God's way. But the Gospel doesn't just save us from our sins and promise life beyond death. The good news of Jesus transforms our current reality as well. In fact, this very story of Jesus (the Son of God) coming to Earth to save us, is a story about community.

Think about it. God himself exists in community—in the Father, the Son (Jesus) and the Holy Spirit. It's a mystery, but, somehow, God exists as three persons in one.

We see this fact in Genesis 1, when God says, "Let us make man in our image, after our likeness." It's an "our" and a "we" from the beginning. God represents relationship and togetherness.

And because God designed us in his image, he wishes us to experience this community as well. He wants us to be right in our relationships with others—and with him. This is why the good news of the Gospel is so important.

The fall of man in Genesis Chapter 3, and the tragic events to follow in the Old Testament, are meant to prepare us for the coming of Christ. When Jesus returns to Earth, our hope for a new humanity—one with restored relationships and without the brokenness of sin—will be realized, with God and with each other.

How exactly will that play out? Let's take another look at the breakdowns in healthy communities throughout the centuries, this time through the lens of the Gospel.

REDEFINING OUR VALUE

One consequence of the fall was not merely an alienation from our neighbors, but the fallout was so severe that it resulted in an alienation even within ourselves.

In other words, in our sin and separation from God, we lost our sense of value and worth. And here's the thing—even as believers, we can still forget those truths. We do this when we allow the world, or our successes and failures, or some other arbitrary source to define us. And usually this leads us to being too distracted, disinterested, or disheartened to pursue community.

As pastor and author Peter Scazzero often says, "We cannot give what we don't already possess." But gazing inwardly for those resources will lead us to base our value on our own judgments and expectations, setting us up for a constant cycle of failure.

Instead, we must rest in the truth of the gospel. The first steps toward genuine community will require you to look away from yourself—and toward God.

When we do this, we discover that our value has already been declared to us by the one who matters most—our Creator. We remember that our identity and value begin with looking at what God says about us. And it turns out that God has a lot to say!

Here are just a few of the things Scripture has to say about those who have trusted in Christ as their Savior:

- You were chosen before the foundations of the world (Ephesians 1)

- You were adopted into God's family (Ephesians 1)

- You were created in his image (Genesis 1)

- You are perfectly loved (1 John 4)

- He desired for you to be forgiven of your sins and spend eternity with him (1 Peter)

- He sent his Son, Jesus, to die for you (John 3)

- In Christ, he calls you a son or a daughter (1 John 3)

- And there is nothing in heaven or on earth that can separate us from God's love (Romans 8)

See? When God sees you—when he gazes at you—he loves you. Immeasurably, fully, and eternally.

And what's even more—God likes you.

Read that sentence again. It's true—he really likes you and wants you to enjoy a meaningful relationship with him. Not only to be saved by him, but to know him. Not only to obey him, but to rest deeply in him.

In fact, he so greatly wants these things for you that he gave his only Son to die a sacrificial death on the cross to make it possible.

This is what Jesus himself says to his disciples before his betrayal, arrest, and crucifixion: "This is my commandment, that you love one another as I have loved you. Greater love has no one than this, that someone lay down his life for his friends" (John 15:12-13).

The sacrificial love displayed in Christ is not just the heart of the gospel—it's the heart of how God loves us.

This is what's behind verses like Romans 5:8, which tells us, "God shows his love for us in that while we were still sinners, Christ died for us."

And the most famous Bible verse of all, John 3:16: "For God so loved the world, that he gave his only Son, that whoever believes in him might not perish but have eternal life."

Catch that—the verse begins with, "For God so loved the world." It's not, "God gave his only Son so that he could love the world." No, God's love for the world—that means you—was there from the beginning of time.

God loved you so much that he gave his Son to die a brutal death for you, in your place. The cross is not just a symbol of payment for sins. It is proof of this life-changing truth:

God loves you. And he has come for you. This is the message of the gospel. Do you believe it?

If you do, then it completely redefines your value. You are incredibly, eternally loved and valued by the Creator of the universe. He says you matter. He says you have a divine purpose.

If those things are true, then you certainly have something to offer those around you. Even if you can't think of anything right off the top of your head, the message that God loves and values us is something worth sharing with others.

Do you think you have a neighbor, coworker, or friend who might need to hear this profound truth?

And if you don't believe this to be true, we invite you to come and see and experience the love of Jesus. At the back of this book, you'll find resources to learn more about what it means to trust in and follow Jesus. We pray the LORD would give you grace to turn from a life of self-reliance and embrace Jesus as Lord and Savior of your life. We'd love to hear from you and help you on that journey.

Allowing the gospel to define our identity and value gives us the motivation and message to reach those around us. If God could love someone like me and you, he can love anybody. That's good news that everyone needs to hear.

REDEFINING OUR SECURITY

No doubt, understanding our value and worth in God's eyes should inspire in us a greater sense of security. After all, if God really does love and want the best for us, that should calm a lot of our anxiety about life and the world.

Still, we think there's another truth that can be easily missed, but that changes our view of community in significant ways.

God loves your neighbor as much as he loves you.

Yes—even if your neighbors are really weird, even if your neighbors make way too much noise, even if your neighbors vote for a different political party, and even if your neighbors aren't Christians—God loves them all. He wants each of them to come to know him, and the hope he has for their lives.

This radical and all-encompassing love that God has for all of humanity is made perfectly clear through the story of the life and the love of Jesus. Many times, during his ministry on Earth, Jesus genuinely shocked people (including his disciples) with his unconditional love toward those considered undeserving—the sinners, the liars, the cheaters, the unfaithful, the sick, the poor, and the disgraced.

Luke writes of these people in his Gospel account:

"Then Levi held a great banquet for Jesus at his house, and a large crowd of tax collectors and others were eating with them. But the Pharisees and the teachers of the law who belonged to their sect complained to his disciples, 'Why do you eat and drink with tax collectors and sinners?'" (Luke 5:29-30)

Notice the writer's description of the group present at Levi's house: "a large crowd of tax collectors and others." Tax collectors were notorious enemies of the people in Jesus' day, known for cheating and stealing from people. As for the others crowded into the house—who were these people?

We don't know for sure, but we do know what the Pharisees thought of them. This group of people Luke referred to as "others," the Pharisees considered "sinners."

"Why do you eat and drink with tax collectors and sinners?" That's their question for Jesus. How could you possibly be associated with these people—the worst of the worst, the enemies of the people?

Jesus' response to these religious teachers is amazing. He makes clear his mission here on Earth, and it's not to make the religiously prideful feel comfortable.

The Bible says: *"Jesus answered them, 'It is not the healthy who need a doctor, but the sick. I have not come to call the righteous, but sinners to repentance.'"* (Luke 5:31-32)

Here, the Son of God declares that he was born not to promote the self-righteous or to seek out those following God's law. His mission is to engage the sick, the sinners, and the others.

Now, before we come down too hard on the Pharisees, let's put ourselves in their shoes. After all, they were the ones attempting (although with far from ideal motives) to follow God's Word. They taught Scripture, and sought to uphold the Bible's commandments and practice its doctrine—in the temple and in the community.

Here, Jesus makes his mission clear. He is keeping company with those in need of spiritual healing, like the tax collectors—egregiously sinful and ungodly people. How could that be? No doubt, the Pharisees would have been shocked, offended, bewildered, and left wondering, "Just what does this Jesus mean?"

If we, today, believe we don't do the same, we're not being honest with ourselves. Who are your others today? Who are the people you don't feel comfortable around and with whom you would never consider associating?

Maybe it's the homeless or the poor. Maybe it's greedy businessmen. Maybe it's criminals or, perhaps, a fallen ministry leader. Maybe it's the neighbor who lives a completely different lifestyle than you. Maybe it's a Democrat or a Republican. Maybe it's millennials, or baby boomers. It might even be Chiefs' fans. (Yes, we're Broncos supporters here.)

Whoever your others are, just imagine coming home to find Jesus sharing a meal with them in your dining room. These people, of whom you think so much less, and who seem the least receptive to the teachings of God, are enjoying a meal with Jesus, who has welcomed them, and is talking with, connecting with, and embracing them.

What would be your immediate reaction? Probably, like the Pharisees, you'd most likely ask the same question. "Why are you hanging out with these people, Jesus?"

The truth is, Jesus knows that we are all broken. We are all sick. We are all in need of a savior.

When Jesus tells the Pharisees he is here for the sick and needy, what the Pharisees miss is that he's not just referring to the tax collectors and the others present. He's referring to the Pharisees as well. In fact, because of their self-righteousness and feelings of exclusivity, they likely need the lion's share of spiritual healing in the room!

The Pharisees can't see it, and don't want to see it. All they recognize is their effort to be godly, and what they perceive to be the lack of effort from everyone else in the room. They have created a clear moral hierarchy in their minds, and have placed themselves at the tip-top. The tax collectors and sinners? They have no business being there.

When we exclude the others in our lives, and adhere to our own moral hierarchy, with ourselves proudly at the summit, we are no different from these religious hypocrites.

James writes about this in the New Testament:

"My brothers, show no partiality as you hold the faith in our Lord Jesus Christ, the Lord of glory. For if a man wearing a

gold ring and fine clothing comes into your assembly, and a poor man in shabby clothing also comes in, and if you pay attention to the one who wears the fine clothing and say, 'You sit here in a good place,' while you say to the poor man, 'You stand over there,' or, 'Sit down at my feet,' have you not then made distinctions among yourselves and become judges with evil thoughts? Listen, my beloved brothers, has not God chosen those who are poor in the world to be rich in faith and heirs of the kingdom, which he has promised to those who love him?" (James 2:1-5)

You see, God knows our hearts completely. He knows that we are just as sick in our flesh as the others upon whom we look down. As followers of Jesus, the only thing that separates us from them is that we have come to know and trust in God's redemptive grace for us through Jesus. That's it!

We aren't better, holier, stronger, or more awesome than anyone else. We're just forgiven.

And forgiven people are forgiving people.

When we look at our neighbors, coworkers, friends, and even those who are other, we need to be reminded that, at the heart level, they truly are no different from us. They are loved by God, and God desires that they know him and experience meaningful community.

This reality should encourage us to accept the others, not scorn them. We should be motivated to move in the direction of the people who seem most opposed to us. Why? Because that's exactly what Jesus did for us. He came to save the lost, lonely, and needy. He came to heal the sick.

Because we are so greatly loved and have been so greatly forgiven, we can be secure in that reality, and unafraid to invite anyone and everyone into it with us. And we can be gracious with those who hurt or offend us.

There is nothing to fear when the God of the universe loves us and the people around us. When we understand God's grace, we are privileged to become the conduit through which he shows that same grace and love to them.

And when we do so, we make it clear just how much God values each one of us.

REDEFINING OPTIMISM

Perhaps nothing is in shorter supply today than optimism. Think about it. Between the political climate, the cultural climate, the economic climate, and the, well, climate climate, bad news and pessimism are pervasive in our culture. All you need to do is turn on the news, read the newspaper, or make a few clicks on the internet or social media, and you'll find that the general feeling about our world is one of hyper-negativity.

A study by Gallup found that Americans are the most stressed-out people in the world. In that study, 55% of Americans said they were stressed, compared with just 35% of the rest of the world. Another 22% of Americans said they regularly feel angry.[22]

There are many sources of this stress and anger: relationships, jobs, familylives, worldviews, economics, politics, etc. We are bombarded with bad news on both a global and personal level.

What is the defining characteristic of the human experience in all these areas? A lack of control. A feeling that we can't do anything about what's broken in our lives and in the world.

While there is some truth to that, there is also truth in the fact that we can make a difference and a change in our lives and the lives of others.

The word optimism is defined as "hopefulness and confidence about the future, or about the successful outcome of something." Perhaps an even better definition is the philosophical one: "the doctrine that this world is the best of all possible worlds."[23]

We love that second definition because it puts forth a novel idea: gratitude. Sure, this world has its problems. But if it's the best of all the possible worlds, we have reason to be grateful, right?

This echoes God's words in Genesis when he creates the Heavens and the Earth, and the plants and animals and birds—and man and woman. And God declares that all of this is "very good."

Then sin is introduced and shakes the world to its core, but the very foundation of the Earth and all God created is still very good.

Even after the devastating events in Genesis 3, the Bible still has much to say about what we can be grateful for.

David, in Psalm 139: 13-14, reflects on the good works of God:

"For you created my inmost being; you knit me together in my mother's womb. I praise you because I am fearfully and wonderfully made; your works are wonderful, I know that full well."

The prophet Jeremiah does the same in Jeremiah 32:17, *"Ah, Sovereign Lord, you have made the heavens and the earth by your great power and outstretched arm. Nothing is too hard for you."*

In 1 Corinthians 1, Paul tells us that God is very much still with us, comforting us when we suffer. *"Praise be to the God and Father of our Lord Jesus Christ, the Father of compassion and the God of all comfort, who comforts us in all our troubles, so that we can comfort those in any trouble with the comfort we ourselves receive from God."*

Best of all, we know that in Jesus, we have been given new life and redemption from our sins. What more could we ask for?

As followers of Jesus, we have every reason in the world (and beyond) to be thankful. And as a result of that gratitude, we become more optimistic. This is a reality desperately needed by the world right now. Hope. Optimism. Courage for the future. We have been given these gifts by Jesus. Let's share them with our neighbors.

REDEFINING JOY

When was the last time you experienced true joy? Not just a fleeting sense of happiness or pleasure, but deep, lasting, all-consuming joy? For most of us, it can feel like joy is in very short supply.

Most often, we likely feel joy when remembering specific moments in our lives, such as our wedding day, the birth of a child, or finding out we got the job or promotion we were desperately hoping for.

The thing about *true* joy is that it's deeper, and more complex and long-lasting, than any of these specific experiences.

Again, let's look to God's Word for some help.

Here's what James 1:2-4 says: *"Count it all joy, my brothers, when you meet trials of various kinds, for you know that the testing of your faith produces steadfastness. And let steadfastness have its full effect, that you may be perfect and complete, lacking in nothing."*

In Philippians 4, Paul writes that we should *"rejoice in the Lord always; again I will say, rejoice."* This comes on the heels of what he wrote in Philippians 3, that the Christian life is a "straining" and that we will face the "enemies of Christ."

It's interesting that in the Bible, joy is often connected to suffering, hardship, and difficulties. The amazing and confounding reality in Scripture is that we are called to be joyful even when experiencing great hardship. It's as if one can't exist without the other.

This is difficult for us to wrap our minds around in a culture that glorifies happiness and idolizes contentment and convenience. The truth is, we all recognize how fleeting those things can be. When we search for happiness through our relationships, jobs, money, successes, travels, or anything else, it will simply not last.

Lasting joy comes from a deeper place, springing from a full understanding that life is about more than the things around which we often organize our daily efforts. There's a greater purpose in life than buying into what culture sells us.

Joy and sorrow are closely related in the Bible. As Pastor Timothy Keller said, "the opposite of joy isn't sorrow; it's hopelessness." In other words, it's possible to experience both joy and sorrow at the same time and still have hope.

We're not talking the kind of joy spread by Mr. Rogers (though we do love Mr. Rogers and, especially, his love for his neighbors.) This joy involves a deep understanding of both the good and the hard in life, and the ability to be joyful and sorrowful at the same time. To *rejoice with those who rejoice, and weep with those who weep."* (Romans 12:15)

This is a perspective that will turn your world (and your neighborhood) upside down. It's the kind of thing that will make people notice something different about you.

Imagine having a conversation with a neighbor who asks you how you've been. Instead of the typical "Good!" response, you answer authentically.

"Well, if I'm being honest, it's been hard lately."

"Really? How come?"

"It feels like my wife and I have no time for each other. We're ships passing in the night. The kids haven't been sleeping well, which means we've been sleeping even worse. And work is becoming more stressful every day."

"That's a lot."

"Yeah, it is. But you know what? We're still joyful."

"Joyful?"

"Yeah. Joyful. Because we know God is at work through all of this. It's hard, but also good and beautiful. And we know we'll make it to the other side."

That kind of genuine joy will stop neighbors in their tracks and make them wonder, "how is that possible?" It's an affirmation that there's joy found in a place of deep conviction and faith, not merely from pleasant circumstances. It is joy that transforms the way you see your life and the people around you.

STORIES FROM THE FRONT

Ty: Have you ever been running and given a total stranger a high-five as you pass one another? I have done it many times. It seems to instantly spark joy.

For someone who grew up in South Dakota (where we all knew one another), waving to anyone who drives by is pretty normal for me. However, I don't expect many people do this. But giving a simple wave or head nod to those who drive or walk by can often bring smiles to their faces. It says to them, "Hey, I see you!"

One of my favorite "Hey I see you" moments occurred in my front yard on a hot summer day while mowing the lawn. Our lawn mower is not an ordinary lawn mower. It came with the house unexpectedly...and for good reason. This gem requires an extension cord to operate. Yep—an extension cord that I have to plug into an electrical outlet.

To this day, it still makes me self-conscious about mowing the lawn. However, our front and back lawns are so tiny that the cord length works perfectly with the one outlet on our front stoop, as well as the one outlet in the back, so we still use it. It has also created a few good laughs between my wife and me.

Anyway, I was convinced that I must be the only person in our neighborhood who used an extension cord to operate his mower. However, on this day, out walked my across-the-street neighbor. Amazingly, his mower used an extension cord, too! There were no words exchanged between the two of us, but our mutual grins and head nods to one another resulted in a funny—and priceless—connection. We were saying, "Hey, I see you're still rocking that electric lawn mower!"

As funny as it sounds, I feel much more comfortable having a conversation with him today because of that interaction. It doesn't take much effort (or many words) to spark joy and open the door to more conversations.

FINDING HUMILITY

There's one more subject we feel the need to highlight when it comes to creating community in our neighborhoods: humility.

Andrew Murray, in his fantastic book, *Humility: The Journey Toward Holiness,* writes, *"Pride must die in you, or nothing of Heaven can live in you."*

For followers of Jesus, this is a significant reminder *and* warning. There is very little good we can do on this Earth, in our neighborhoods, in our churches, or in our homes, without the cessation of our pride. In other words, humility is incredibly important.

Look around your world today. How much humility do you see? How often do you hear of someone putting another person ahead of themselves, a politician deferring to another, an employee suggesting that a co-worker receive a raise instead of him, or a person willingly and readily admitting their faults and struggles?

These things tend to be so rare that, when we do hear about them, they resonate as surprisingly as hearing about a snowstorm in Las Vegas would. We are all amazed and encouraged by stories like this.

But why are they so uncommon?

The root of this goes back to the story in Genesis 3, and to the reality that sin has broken us and our world. Eve, in the Garden, is tempted to believe that she is endowed with the same understanding as God. What greater temptation could there be for a human?

It was pride, in many ways, that led Adam and Eve to commit the first sins on planet Earth.

Pride destroys community, but humility builds bridges.

In Genesis, Adam and Eve said, "I deserve this...God must be hiding something from me...I know best." Humility would have been expressed as, "Maybe I'm wrong about this. God is God, and I'm not. I should trust his plan because I'm not capable of seeing the big picture."

This kind of humility is transformative in relationships. Would you rather have friends who act like they know everything, or friends who admit their failings and are honest about their struggles? No contest, right?

Your neighbors would certainly prefer you to be a humble person, as well.

What does practicing humility look like?

It means you are willing to have conversations, listen to opposing opinions, and be open to differing belief systems. It means not being quick to judge, not spewing your opinions to the detriment of others. It means not gossiping about others, but focusing instead on the good in everyone. It means not feeling above changing a light bulb for your elderly neighbor, or picking up the deposit left by your neighbor's dog (for the 200th time).

It also means being thoughtful about how you present yourself and your home. It may seem relatively unimportant, but taking good care of your home matters to your neighbors. A sloppy yard with overgrown weeds does nothing to improve your neighborhood's appearance—and can even lower the value of everyone's homes.

Similarly, a yard full of political signs during election season might seem like a great way to share your beliefs and values with the neighborhood. However, keep in mind that politics turns far more people off than it inspires them to change their political minds (see Chapter 3). In fact, posting a political sign may telegraph to your neighbors who support the opposing side that you may not be a level-headed, approachable person. Is that worth a political statement?

It's considerations like these that challenge us to think differently. Put simply, we have to begin to think like Jesus.

Here's how Paul describes Jesus in his plea to the church in Philippi:

"Do nothing from selfish ambition or conceit, but in humility count others more significant than yourselves. Let each of you look not only to his own interests, but also to the interests of others. Have this mind among yourselves, which is yours in Christ Jesus, who, though he was in the form of God,

did not count equality with God a thing to be grasped, but emptied himself, by taking the form of a servant, being born in the likeness of men. And being found in human form, he humbled himself by becoming obedient to the point of death, even death on a cross. Therefore God has highly exalted him and bestowed on him the name that is above every name." (Philippians 2:3-9)

Jesus was who he was—and lived as he lived—because he humbled himself. The call to all followers of Jesus, as Paul makes clear here, is to go and do likewise.

The Bible speaks of humility in many other places as well.

Scripture says: *"God opposes the proud but shows favor to the humble."* (James 4:6)

Want to be on the wrong side of God? Act proudly.

"He has shown you, O mortal, what is good. And what does the Lord require of you? To act justly and to love mercy and to walk humbly with your God." (Micah 6:8)

In other words, God has given us a simple plan of obedience: Be humble, and act with justice and mercy toward others.

"For all those who exalt themselves will be humbled, and those who humble themselves will be exalted." (Luke 14:11)

Jesus once again shows us the significance of humility. Those who humble themselves will be honored by God. Those who fail to humble themselves will face God's humbling process, which likely won't be much fun.

If we want to transform our neighborhoods, if we want to see the Gospel displayed, if we want to build lasting and meaningful relationships, we must grow in humility.

A great place to start is to ask yourself this question: Do you believe you are better than, holier than, or smarter than your neighbors? Is there anything you hold over the heads of your neighbors? If there is, spend some time prayerfully processing these beliefs and asking yourself how you might be humbled as a member of your community.

When you allow your heart and your perspective to be transformed by the Gospel, you are able to act, communicate, and live more openly and honestly.

Your neighbors will recognize it, and doors will open as a result.

CLEANING UP THE PARTY FOULS

In Chapter 4, we explored three of the most common party fouls that splinter relationships and make community more difficult in today's culture; political division, racial tension, and busyness.

Now that we've explored how the Gospel transforms our view of ourselves and others, let's look at each of these areas again to see how we can approach them differently in light of who we can become in Christ:

Cleaning Up Party Foul #1: Politics

The political divisions today are so deeply rooted that overcoming them can feel like a hopeless endeavor.

Yet, if you think about it, you can probably name someone—a family member, friend, co-worker, etc.—who has starkly different political opinions, but with whom you also have a genuine relationship. Maybe it's your aunt, who knows to avoid "that topic" on Thanksgiving; or perhaps it's your neighbor with the crazy bumper stickers on her car. Most of us have found that it's quite possible (and sometimes incredibly rewarding) to have a good relationship with someone despite vehement disagreement on important issues.

Here's the thing. Our political culture—and the media that covers it—wants us to believe that the opposing party is the enemy. Sound familiar? When we are tempted to view others as our enemy, we need to remember Ephesians 6. Our battle is not with flesh and blood, but a powerful, *spiritual* enemy.

Political polarization is great for voter motivation and TV ratings. That's why our political parties and cable news channels want to fuel the fire as best they can. However, when we take time to really see those on the other side of the political fence, have a real conversation with them, make an honest effort to understand their world, and listen to the reasoning behind their beliefs—it can change *everything*.

Studies back this up, showing that Democrats and Republicans with a significant number of friends who are members of the opposing party have less negative feelings toward the party in general.[24]

This idea is by no means new. It's the path Jesus laid out for us in Matthew 5:

"You have heard that it was said, 'You shall love your neighbor and hate your enemy.' But I say to you, love your enemies and pray for those who persecute you, so that you may be sons of your Father who is in heaven. For he makes his sun rise on the evil and on the good, and sends rain on the just and on the unjust. For if you love those who love you, what reward do you have? Do not even the tax collectors do the same? And if you greet only your brothers, what more are you doing than others? Do not even the Gentiles do the same?"

Jesus was the best at loving and engaging people who lived and believed differently. He invented the idea. Remember that he came to live and die for you and for me, even though we are sinners and far from deserving his grace.

The Gospel is all about accepting the undeserving, loving the unlovable, and forgiving the unforgivable.

Here's what happens when we do this: We discover the essence of people. It's a whole lot harder to demonize someone sitting right in front of you—someone with whom you can listen and relate. It's hard to be critical with someone that you care about personally.

Perhaps the best way to solve our political divisions is to follow Jesus' example of getting to know, and accepting, and loving, our politically different neighbors.

Cleaning Up Party Foul #2: The Racial Divide

As we now know, Paul, in the book of Ephesians, challenges us to think differently about the Church because of the ultimate sacrifice made by Jesus on the cross.

We are one—in the Church and in Jesus. It doesn't matter our culture, class, gender, race, or political ideals. We are meant to be united by this life-changing philosophy, the most important thing on Earth.

But, do our churches actually practice that principle?

Simply put, as Christians we must be willing to love and welcome those with any and all differences into the

Church if we ever expect to be able to genuinely relate with our neighbors.

How do we do this? It's going to look different in every context. Many churches find themselves in a community that is far from racially diverse.

Do you make a point to find people in your church who look different, and ask about their stories? Is your church considering ways to reach out to, and relate to, different populations in your community, and not just the ones who are represented by the majority in your fellowship? Is there a congregation nearby with a different racial makeup that you could partner with in ministry?

As followers of Jesus, we have an incredible opportunity to present a powerful picture of what unity, diversity, and compassion can look like between human beings.

It is what God has called us all to be, and it is through the Gospel that it is made possible.

Cleaning Up Party Foul #3: Busyness

Whether we want to admit it or not, busyness is a major player when it comes to our ability to build and maintain meaningful relationships in our lives. So how do we address this challenge?

Again, the Gospel helps us reorient our thinking. Remember that, through Jesus, God has re-welcomed us into his family and given us a place to belong—regardless of our sins, and in spite of our failings.

Hebrews 13:2 is one of the more mind-bending verses in the New Testament. It says, *"Do not forget to show hospitality to strangers, for by so doing some people have shown hospitality to angels without knowing it."*

In other words, we never truly know the power or the significance of showing hospitality to others. And, as the Bible says, we may even experience something heavenly as a result. If opening up to your neighbors seems difficult, maybe it's time to simply welcome them in. One practical way to get past the busyness dilemma is to think about how you might be able to invite others into the regular rhythms of your life.

Do you have friends over every Friday night for tacos? Invite a neighbor to join you next time. Does your kid have a soccer game on Saturday morning? See if the widow down the street would enjoy coming along to watch kids run around chaotically on a field. Need advice or help with a landscaping project? Maybe that gentleman who's in his yard every time you drive past would be willing to offer advice or lend a hand.

In other words, when you stop focusing on creating time to reach out to your neighbors and, instead, invite them to share in the regular, mundane events in your life, you might be surprised to find how simple it is. You may be shocked at how willing he or she is to step into that space with you.

Along the way, you might discover a greater purpose in the things that often make you feel so busy.

GETTING BACK ON TRACK

While reading this book, maybe you've come to the realization that you've strayed from the ways and words of Jesus, and are now convinced that you haven't been living in a Christ-like way toward those around you. Or maybe you are hearing and considering some of these truths for the first time, and realizing how far you seem to be from the rewarding experience of relationship and community.

Perhaps you've had significant conflicts with your neighbors, or with others in your life. Maybe thinking about reaching out makes your body tense and your heart race. The hurt we experience from others is real, and the anxiety can be paralyzing. It can feel impossible to move forward, to forgive and be forgiven, to make relationships right again.

Well, we've got good news for you, because the Gospel isn't just a one-time, limited offer. It's a powerful, never-ending message—a well that never runs dry. And we can (and should) return to it over and over again to strengthen our faith and replenish our spirit.

The story of the Prodigal Son is one of Jesus' most famous parables—one he told to enlighten people about the Kingdom of God, and about God's eternal love for all of us. It is found in Luke 15. It's well worth reading again and again, because everything we've been talking about can be found in it:

"And (Jesus) said, "There was a man who had two sons. And the younger of them said to his father, 'Father, give me the share of property that is coming to me.' And he divided his property between them. Not many days later, the younger son gathered all he had and took a journey into a far country, and there he squandered his property in reckless living. And when he had spent everything, a severe famine arose in that country, and he began to be in need. So he went and hired himself out to one of the citizens of that country, who sent him into his fields to feed pigs. And he was longing to be fed with the pods that the pigs ate, and no one gave him anything."

"And he said, 'How many of my father's hired servants have more than enough bread, but I perish here with hunger! I will arise and go to my father, and I will say to him, Father, I have sinned against heaven and before you. I am no longer worthy to be called your son. Treat me as one of your hired servants.' And he arose and came to his

father. But while he was still a long way off, his father saw him and felt compassion, and ran and embraced him and kissed him. And the son said to him, 'Father, I have sinned against heaven and before you. I am no longer worthy to be called your son.' But the father said to his servants, 'Bring quickly the best robe, and put it on him, and put a ring on his hand, and shoes on his feet. And bring the fattened calf and kill it and let us eat and celebrate. For this my son was dead, and is alive again; he was lost, and is found.' And they began to celebrate." (Luke 15:11-24)

Catch that? This father—whose son rejected him and abandoned him—is ready with open arms to receive him when he returns. But he doesn't punish his son. He says, "Let's party!" There is meant to be a celebration when we humbly admit our faults and reclaim who we were made to be.

Jesus' story makes clear the kind of love God has for us. We are so often like that younger son, who chooses his own way and ends up in trouble because of it.

But like the good father in the story, God never forgets about us. He waits for us. And when we repent, and return to him—back to our true home—he is always and forever ready to receive us. He is ready to come running to embrace us when we are "still a long way off."

If you feel as though you are a long way off, know that God has great compassion for you. He will forgive you, and provide you the ability to forgive others.

God is always ready to welcome you back into his community—the home where you belong.

And when we run back into his arms, there will be a party.

It's kind of his thing.

RESHAPING CHURCH AND CULTURE

Of course, there's one other major challenge that stands in the way of this vision of redemption and acceptance that we haven't really discussed. We are not in control.

It's clear that we can't completely control what happens around us, particularly when it comes to changes within our culture or even the Church.

As we've seen, our culture is becoming less and less inclined to view the Church and religion as a good or necessary thing. People are less inclined to view Christianity or the Church capable of answering their biggest questions and responding to their most challenging needs. Even the Church community has become more challenged by the advent of technology, online services, and divisive issues within the Christian body itself.

We would love to say that all this is going to get better, that things are looking up, and that it's all going to be one giant, rosy symphony of community. In truth, we really don't know how things will look up until the day Jesus returns. (And on that day, we will all look up—literally.)

Until that day, it's probably safe to assume that things will continue to be challenging when it comes to healing our culture. The world will, most likely, continue tearing us away from each other, rather than encouraging us to develop meaningful relationships.

Within this reality, however, comes our greatest motivation. If we can learn to be life-givers, joy-sparkers, and community-builders right where we are, we will be inspired to make positive differences in our neighborhoods for the rest of our lives.

As the culture becomes more divided, we can be beacons of unity.

As our country becomes more anti-religion, we can show the love of Jesus in creative ways—beyond the walls of church buildings.

As the Church becomes less connected, we can remind our brothers and sisters in Christ who we are called to be, and show them the way back to being a family again.

For all of us, as parents, grandparents, or perhaps parents-to-be, we can, someday, pass on the gift of hopeful community that will spread through the generations to come.

If this all feels a bit overwhelming, let these two writers remind you that your hope is rooted in the power of Jesus. We don't have any answers in and of ourselves. Instead, as we look to the power of the Cross, and the ministry of Christ, we will find the blueprint for transforming our world with his love.

The Gospel is both the message and the means by which to begin rebuilding community in our world.

Here are a few things to remember as you think about what this looks like in your life.

Small steps make a big difference. The baked goods you deliver to your neighbor will be remembered for, at minimum, days (but more likely for weeks, months, even years). Try taking a small step and see what happens.

Every day presents a new opportunity to try again. That's the beauty of building community with our neighbors. You're always going to have them—unless you move to Antarctica (*Party in the Front: Antarctica!* coming soon). This means that you'll never lack opportunities to love, serve, listen, and pray. Each day brings a whole new world of possibilities to your street. Even better, God's mercy is reborn every day.

Ultimately, this mission isn't just ours; it's God's. It's the mission Jesus gave to his disciples in Matthew 28—to go forth and make plenteous the followers of Jesus. To show and teach people what it means to know and follow Him. To bring the light of the world to the ends of the Earth.

The message at the heart of Scripture is to love your God and love your neighbors. When a religious teacher asks Jesus what he considers the greatest commandment in Scripture, Jesus responds:

"And he said to him, 'You shall love the Lord your God with all your heart and with all your soul and with all your mind. This is the great and first commandment.' And in a second response Jesus says, 'You shall love your neighbor as yourself. On these two commandments depend all the Law and the Prophets.'" (Matthew 22:37-40)

Love your neighbor as yourself. This is what partying in the front is all about.

It's the foundation upon which community is built. It's seeing yourself and others justly. It's knowing your value, sharing your optimism and joy, and remaining humble through all of it.

As you follow Jesus, you can trust that he will lead you—and empower you—to recognize the path he has chosen for you, and to love the people he has placed in your life. You can also trust him to transform the lives of those around you in his way and in his time.

And along the journey, he'll be transforming you, too.

CHAPTER 6

A VISION FOR THE FUTURE

"There is nothing in the world so good as good neighbors." —Laura Ingalls Wilder

---

STORIES FROM THE FRONT

Ty: We were relatively new to our neighborhood. During that short time, however, we had already experienced the joys of community with our fellow residents. Recently, I was reminded of our (actually everyone's) need for community, and was very grateful for much-needed help from our neighbors.

Late one night, we received the sad news that my wife's father had died unexpectedly. We decided it would be best for my wife to drive back to our hometown to help with some of the planning, which left me at home with four of our five children. (Side note: Being responsible for the kids—alone—is a great reminder to me of all the hard work my wife does at home.)

I am so grateful for the ways in which our sweet new neighbors encouraged us. Our children began asking

---

if they could play out front, where they could see their new friends. So, after nap time the next afternoon, we went out to see if other kids were playing in their front yards. Our neighbors across the street (who also have five children) were just walking outside. I told the parents what had happened to my father-in-law, and they invited us to walk to the park with them. We had a great time, and ended up playing pick-up football on the playground.

An hour later, our kids and I walked back inside our home smiling, and I was incredibly encouraged. It was time to make supper, and I realized that I had forgotten to buy cheese that morning for our quesadillas.

The last thing I wanted to do was pack up four kids (age seven and under) to go to the grocery store just to buy cheese. Thankfully, we had recently met a sweet family down the street, and you guessed it! They had cheese. And they were happy to help this (obviously) struggling dad. (Shout out again to my amazing wife who plans, shops for, and prepares meals every day for our army at home.)

These simple, yet impactful, gestures from our neighbors may not have been so forthcoming had we not hosted a Saturday front-lawn breakfast block party a month earlier. It was amazing to witness the ripening fruit of those block party conversations. I suddenly felt the freedom to be vulnerable with these sweet neighbors, and to ask for help in a time of need.

OUT IN FRONT

What's the best thing about a party? Maybe for you it's the cupcakes. Or the streamers. Or the party favors. Or the gifts.

Whatever it is, we think the best thing about a party is the fun. The fact is, at a party, what's so often hidden inside of us in everyday life comes pouring out—joy, enthusiasm, smiles, laughter.

Parties have a unique power to transport us back to our childhoods. It's no secret that kids are great at partying. In fact, sometimes they don't even need an actual party to party. (Have you ever seen a four-year-old at bedtime? It's a party. It's always a party.) We adults have a harder time partying spontaneously. It almost always takes a special occasion of some sort to bring out the joy and happiness in us.

That's exactly what we're getting at when we talk about partying in the front. It's not just about what events you can pull off in your neighborhood (though events can be great). It's about bringing you—the real you—to the table so that others have the opportunity to really get to know you.

It's about letting others see and share your joy—and your sorrows. Your highs and your lows. Your good days and your bad ones.

It's about allowing people to experience a deeper relationship with you so that you might touch their lives in meaningful ways. In return, they just might do the same for you.

A Man Called Otto (2022), directed by and starring Tom Hanks, is a remake of the Swedish film, *A Man Called Ove*, based on the novel of the same name by Fredrik Backman.

In the story, Otto is a grouchy, disillusioned older man who resides in the Pittsburgh suburbs. He has lived alone since the loss of his beloved wife years before. The story opens in a shocking fashion, with Otto preparing to take his own life. He has—simply put—had enough.

Otto's plan to end his life is continually and hilariously interrupted by his new neighbors, a married couple with two young daughters. These new neighbors are at a complete loss as they move in and settle down. Otto really has no choice but to help them out.

These new neighbors come to Otto's front door for this or that, over and over. Otto's resentment towards, and frustration with, the family slowly—but surely—changes from exasperation to understanding and acceptance. He even (gasp) babysits the couple's children so that they can have a date night.

Through this neighborly connection, Otto's life is not only saved, but is also remade with purpose and joy. What stands out in the movie is just how simple this process is. Tommy and Marisol move in with their kids. They ask Otto for help. They bring over a dish for dinner. They say hello to him when they see him.

Then life just happens—continuing to provide opportunities for Otto and his neighbors (all of whom freely choose to move toward each other) to connect. And a remarkable bond begins to grow.

At the start of the story, Otto seems the kind of man who is unlikely to be changed—by anything. By the end, he is a completely different person. The joy has returned. The laughter is back. The kid in him starts making appearances again.

And if you think this is a fairytale story, we've got stats to back up the reality of it. Just remember that the US Surgeon General declared an epidemic of loneliness, and stated that loneliness is worse for your health than smoking 15 cigarettes daily.

Well, there's a flip side to those statistics as well—a positive side. A 2010 study, which followed over 300,000 people, presented findings that showed those with strong social connections—community—can increase their likelihood of survival by 50%.[25] As the study explains, "this means that by the time half of a hypothetical sampling of 100 people have died, there will be five people who will likely live longer, thanks to stronger social relationships."

Notably, this report looked specifically at all social relationships—not just marriage or family connections. In other words, whether you are married, single, living near family or not, meaningful community is life-giving.

Getting to know your neighbors isn't just a really nice idea, it's an undeniable health benefit! Want to live longer? Celebrate community.

We hope this gives you an idea of what is possible in your neighborhood. Sure, A Man Called Otto is a Hollywood story. But it can be your story as well. Maybe by utilizing simple, practical steps, we can create relationships, and spark life-changing community right where we are.

We believe it's possible.

But as is true with anything worth having or accomplishing, these things don't just magically happen on its own.

It takes effort. It requires consistency. It means overcoming those feelings of anxiety and fear, and making a real effort to move toward others.

It takes a willingness to let your true self be seen—to be a little bit of a kid again. And it means being less concerned about what others think and, instead, simply enjoying being with people.

But here's the good news: while it does take effort, it really is not as scary or as difficult as you may envision. Because once you get started, the party begins to build momentum.

One act of kindness toward a neighbor will fuel another, and then another. And before you know it, you've created a community snowball effect.

One afternoon spent sitting on your front porch could result in a spontaneous conversation that becomes a friendship that turns into a real connection.

One pancake breakfast might just morph into a neighborhood tradition, transforming the way your neighbors see themselves and experience relationships with others.

One lemonade stand could brighten someone's day, inspire more families to do the same, and bring loads of joy (and sugar!) to the people around you.

What might this idea look like in your neighborhood? What steps can you take?

Let us give you some tools for building profound community relationships right where you are.

BLESS YOUR NEIGHBORS

One of the most helpful strategies we've found when it comes to reaching out to your neighbors is what's known as BLESS. This philosophy is not the title of a Hallmark movie or the linchpin of a Hobby Lobby campaign. It's actually an incredibly helpful (and practical) tool.

Utilized by the Christian leadership organization, Verge Network, it has been utilized by churches and Christians as a practical guide—a blueprint—for how to love our neighbors well.[26]

Here's what BLESS stands for:

B—Begin with Prayer

L—Listen

E—Eat

S—Serve

S—Share

This strategy has helped us and our families take that important first step toward reaching out to our neighbors.

B (BEGIN WITH PRAYER)

How often do you pray for your neighbors? Or does that seem like a completely odd idea? Paul believed deeply that starting with prayer was essential to missional living. He writes about it in Colossians.

"Continue steadfastly in prayer, being watchful in it with thanksgiving. At the same time, pray also for us, that God may open to us a door for the word, to declare the mystery of Christ, on account of which I am in prison—that I may make it clear, which is how I ought to speak. Walk in wisdom toward outsiders, making the best use of the time. Let your speech always be gracious, seasoned with salt, so that you may know how you ought to answer each person." (Colossians 4:2-6)

There is a bunch of good stuff in these verses about how to share the Gospel with the world—by being watchful, being thankful, speaking with clarity, walking with wisdom in relation to those around you, making the best use of your time, etc. Still, it all begins with prayer.

Paul asks the Colossian Christians to pray for him. To pray that God would "open to us a door for the Word." Paul—the first, and probably most important, missionary in the New Testament and the young Christian church—knows that he can't simply make mission happen. He can't just start knocking on doors and hope for the best. He can't rely only on his intelligence, religious training, or dashing good looks (actually, we don't know what Paul looked like, so scratch that last one).

Paul relied on prayer. He asked God—and invited the Colossians to join him—to reveal to Paul where He wanted him to go. Paul asked that He "open to us a door" to enable the Gospel to be received.

If Paul really felt this, and conducted himself this way, shouldn't we do the same? We need to recognize that God is sovereign—completely in control of our lives and our world. He knows who he wants us to reach, and when, and why.

And it all starts with asking God for help.

Here's the thing. To start praying for your neighbors, you need to know who they are. You need to know how best to pray for them.

Is there a couple with young kids? Is someone divorced, and struggling as a single parent? Has a family moved in that is new to the area? Has an older couple downsized after years of living elsewhere? Are parents employed? Retired? What are their hobbies and interests? What foods do they especially enjoy?

These are all very simple things to start paying attention to so that you can pray for them more effectively, and better understand how to BLESS them in the future.

Here's an idea to try. Print out a Google Satellite map of your neighborhood and write the names of your neighbors on their homes. Then post it in an obvious place for easy reference. Once you do this, begin making notes about your neighbors names, likes, dislikes, habits, hobbies, the things they enjoy, etc. Writing "loves chocolate cupcakes" next to a neighbor's name gives you an incredible advantage when he or she needs a pick-me-up somewhere down the road. Realizing that you actually remember they shared this fact with you will mean the world to them.

This will help you to remember to pray for your neighbors and will serve as a motivational reminder to get to know the ones you haven't met. It can be somewhat eye-opening to practice this exercise and to realize how many people you don't know a thing about who live within a football's throw of your house.

L (LISTEN)

"Being heard is so close to being loved that, for the average person, they are almost indistinguishable." –David W. Augsburger

That is a powerful quote. It's powerful because it's true. Being really listened to is so significant (and so rare these days), that it can immediately make someone feel loved.

Think about it. When was the last time you felt listened to—really heard? Maybe it was with a friend over a good cup of coffee. Or on a phone conversation with a family member who asked all the right questions. Or maybe it was a meeting with your counselor or spiritual mentor.

When someone listens to you, they affirm you. They affirm that you matter, and that what you're saying, feeling, and thinking are actually important to them. That is an incredibly loving interaction to experience.

The ability to listen is tantamount to a superpower. And it is crucial when it comes to creating community. People are so used to not being listened to that when we genuinely engage and make an effort to really hear them, the result can be revolutionary!

Now, here's the catch. Most people think they are great listeners. (In fact, it's been estimated that 96% of people believe they are.) However, researchers have found that most people only retain around 50% of any conversation. That's a big disconnect!

In our distraction-filled world, the ability to listen is becoming rarer and rarer. A 2010 study by Harvard researchers found that our minds tend to wander about 47% of the time when we are doing anything, including talking to someone.

Some of that is simple human wiring. We're wired to think about how we'll respond. And we tend to relate things we hear to ourselves and our own experiences. That's not all bad.

But, by becoming better listeners, we can build connections and trust in a way that most people can't or won't, or don't know how to.

So, since your mind has probably wandered for roughly 47% of the time it's taken you to read this chapter so far, let's quickly get down to brass tacks. How can we become better listeners?

- Focus on what the person is saying and on the feeling behind it. Don't just hear the words; listen and look for the emotions behind them. Good listening requires an emotional—and a spiritual—presence, not just a physical one. Ask God to help you interpret what is happening in the person's mind and heart.

- Be curious and ask good questions. To be curious is to wonder and ask, "What do they mean by that?" "What do they think about that? "What are the true feelings behind their statements?" Staying curious helps you stay engaged in the conversation. Then actually ask these questions out loud. Rather than feeling challenged, your friend, family member, or work associate is likely to feel grateful. Your questions indicate your genuine interest.

- Repeat statements back to the speaker. Your neighbor might tell you, "I'm feeling discouraged about my relationship with my son." You can show that you're listening (and help yourself stay focused) by saying something like, "Would you like to talk about the relationship? Tell me more about it." You're likely to be amazed by the fact that simply affirming the speaker's feelings can encourage him or her to take the conversation further.

- Write down notes immediately after a conversation. It doesn't need to be a full documentation of every word said (remember, you're only going to remember about half of it anyway!).

Still, jotting down a few important points will help you to pray for them more effectively, and will set you up for success the next time you see them. Remembering what has been hard or good or challenging for someone, and mentioning those things the next time you see that person, will make a big impact. This is way better than seeing your neighbor and saying something like, "Hey, how is old...what's his name, again? You know, your son?" (Not a great look on you.)

If you're not sure how to love your neighbors well, start by just listening to them. You'll be surprised at what you find out and where it takes you.

STORIES FROM THE FRONT

Jeff: My wife Becca has a natural gift for creating hospitality and connection. People just instantly like her. (Hey, I did!) She also has a knack for coming up with simple and powerful ways to build community with people around us.

A few summers back, she decided to invite the neighbors to the park by our house, and she brought along some popsicles. It really didn't take much effort—a few flyers around the neighborhood, a mention to those we saw in the days leading up to the event—but the impact was incredible.

On the evening of the popsicle event, over 70 people showed up. We (just) barely had enough popsicles to go around (thanks to—if I'm honest—a few kids who most likely enjoyed more than one).

In the summers since, our popsicle night has ballooned into a full-fledged neighborhood party. This past summer, over 150 neighbors showed up, along with food trucks and a face painter.

It's amazing how a simple idea can bring so many people together. And it wasn't just the popsicles. It was the result of my wife's open heart and the message received by it—you are seen, you are cared about, you are welcome.

E (EAT)

This might be the most simple and profound element of the BLESS strategy.

Yep, you've got it right. The next step in blessing your neighbors is to share food with them. How awesome is that?

You can't have a great party without good food, right?

The key, of course, is not just to eat, but to eat together in a familial way.

There is something powerful about sharing a meal. Over a meal, walls are broken down and intimacy is created. We're all equal over the dinner table—just ordinary human beings who need some sustenance to survive.

Jesus himself utilized this strategy in his ministry on Earth. Tim Chester, in his fantastic book, *A Meal with Jesus: Discovering Grace, Community, and Mission Around the Table*, notes: *"In Luke's Gospel, Jesus is either going to a meal, at a meal, or coming from a meal."* In fact, Chester cites at least 16 occasions on which Jesus is eating with others, preparing to eat with others, or talking about eating with others.

Why? Jesus used eating together as an avenue to the heart of people. He understood that, in the culture of the day, eating together was an instant sign of connection and community. It was also a way to communicate love.

Here is a scene from the Gospel of Matthew describing how Jesus again broke down the cultural barriers of the day by eating with some interesting company.

"While Jesus was having dinner at Matthew's house, many tax collectors and sinners came and ate with him and his disciples. When the Pharisees saw this, they asked his disciples, 'Why does your teacher eat with tax collectors and sinners?' On hearing this, Jesus said, 'It is not the healthy who need a doctor, but the sick. But go and learn what this means: I desire mercy, not sacrifice. For I have not come to call the righteous, but sinners.'" (Matthew 9:12-13)

At that table with tax collectors, Pharisees, his disciples, and many others, Jesus turned a meal into a mission.

We can do the same. All cultures celebrate through the act of sharing food, and show love the same way. If you want people to feel valued, feed them.

And when you present a meal to them in your home, not only will you (and they) experience community, you will be the beneficiaries of instantly sparked intimacy. People who have been accepted into your home and provided with something to eat have also been invited into a relationship. They may not be instantly won over, but when you share a meal with your friends and neighbors, the opportunity to learn about them, yourself, and the heart of Jesus is realized.

Don't be intimidated by this idea. Hosting someone in your home doesn't mean you have to serve a roast turkey or cook like Guy Fieri. It can be as simple as having someone over for cookies or a cup of coffee. Have you tried good, old-fashioned Oreos and a glass of milk recently? It's like manna from Heaven.

Any way in which you invite people to experience genuine love and meaningful relationships in your home will go a long way toward creating real community with those around you.

If you can hand out a popsicle, you can throw a party in the front.

And you can make a powerful impact in your neighborhood.

S (SERVE)

The first "S" in "BLESS" represents what it means to serve.

Merriam-Webster defines serving as performing a duty or service for another person or an organization. We don't love that definition. Christ-like serving has a very different meaning.

Here's what Scripture has to say about serving:

1 John 4:7 says, *"Beloved, let us love one another, for love is from God, and whoever loves has been born of God and*

knows God. Anyone who does not love does not know God, because God is love."

In other words, you cannot say you love God and fail to love others. The two go hand in hand.

Philippians 2:3 calls us to practice an even more challenging way to love. *"Do nothing out of selfish ambition or vain conceit," Paul writes. "Rather, in humility value others above yourselves."*

As those who have been loved and served and saved by Christ, we are called to put others' needs and wishes before our own. Paul doesn't delineate here by relationship. He doesn't say, "value your spouse above yourself," or "value other Christians before yourself." He says to value "others," as in anyone else you can serve.

So, if that's at the heart of what sacrificial serving is all about, what does it look like in practice?

One of the qualities that can transform any relationship is the willingness to put someone else's needs first. This begins with a change in our hearts and in the way we think.

When you walk outside your front door or drive out of your garage today, pause and ask yourself, "I wonder how my neighbors are doing, and what's going on in their lives? How might I help them with things they need?"

So often, it's easy to stay in our own little world. By the time we're through with our work day or have dropped off the kids at their 7,000th activity of the week, we are laser-focused on getting home and taking care of whatever's next. That's not necessarily a bad thing.

Still, how often do we miss opportunities to engage with our neighbors simply because we aren't thinking about them? Making an effort to think about, and pray about, our neighbors will invite us to pay closer attention to the ways in which we can serve them.

Could your neighbor who is always working on his car use some help on a Saturday? Is the widow who lives next to you needing some yard work done? Could the family that's still battling sickness use a meal, or benefit from you making a grocery store run on their behalf? Putting your neighbors' needs in focus will transform the way you think about your place in their lives.

Yes, it will require a sacrifice of your time and resources, and maybe some of the things you need to get done will be put off for a bit. But that's what serving is all about, right?

You might just find that your sacrificial serving sparks in others the same desire to serve. Perhaps your neighbors will realize the value in helping you, and others, as well.

Everyone has unique gifts to contribute—qualities well suited to serve you and others in your community. Maybe you could engage your handy neighbor to help you with the next electrical issue you come up against, instead of relying on Google and your lucky screwdriver.

Sometimes, letting others serve you is the best way to open the door to relationship building.

Want to blow away your neighbors? Make it a point to find ways to serve them authentically and sacrificially.

S (SHARE)

The second "S" in "BLESS" stands for share—as in share your story.

As we've seen, there are many reasons we find it hard to create community with our neighbors. And cultural and logistical barriers further complicate the issue. But if we're honest with ourselves, one of the biggest reasons we shy away from reaching out to neighbors is that we are simply afraid.

Why are we fearful? Maybe it's the fear that people will really see us, get to know us, and find reasons to reject us. And, no doubt, it's easier to live at a distance from other people, even the people who live within yards of our homes. But even if it is a bit scary to think we might have to talk about who we are and what we believe with those around us, the rewards far outweigh the drawbacks.

This isn't just a theory. A 2020 study by Campus Crusade found that a majority of Christians talk about their faith with fellow believers most of the time. Only about 20% of Christians say they regularly talk to non-believers about the subject. That's a pretty small number. What do you suppose is preventing the other 80% from sharing information about their religion and how it has impacted their lives? Fear. Fear of not having all the answers. Fear of offending someone. Fear of shedding a bad light on Christianity.

These fears are understandable and legitimate. And, unfortunately, there are many examples of Christians sharing their beliefs in ways that are unhelpful and even damaging to the religious community as a whole. We certainly don't want to be added to that list!

Considering that, there's another way to look at sharing our experiences with faith and religion. Imagine meeting a neighbor who has just moved to your street. As you get to know each other, he or she asks you questions about your life (which is perfectly normal, and expected). Imagine not talking about your spouse or kids in these conversations! Okay, maybe it just doesn't come up. Maybe you find that the two of you have a lot of other things to share. Fair enough. Now, imagine that in your next conversation with this neighbor, you still don't share that you're married or that you have children. And on it goes.

Then envision that, at some point, your neighbor finally sees your spouse or your kids out in the yard. He or she is bound to be, at the least, mildly surprised that you never shared information about such a huge part of your life, may even be somewhat offended, and may think, "Why would he not tell me about his family? Is he hiding something from me?"

So, here's the point we're making. If we truly believe that the God of the universe has saved us through his Son, Jesus, and that our relationship with this God influences absolutely everything about our lives—in other words, is a massive part of who we are—to not share that story with others is tantamount to withholding major truths about your family and your life. It just doesn't make sense.

At some point, our neighbors will (or should) recognize our faith. They'll see something different about us. They'll see us dressed up or piling the kids into the minivan on a Sunday morning. They'll notice that every Wednesday night a group of people shows up at our door with Bibles and a potluck item. It'll become obvious that this is a very important part of who we are. If we haven't said anything to them about it, it will probably leave them feeling a little bit strange about us, and wondering why we wouldn't share something so integral to our lives.

Viewing this challenge in such a way puts it in a new light. Our faith—what we believe, what Jesus has helped us realize about our lives, the hope we have in God's plan and purpose—should be of the utmost importance when revealing our authentic selves to others. Even more so than introducing the subjects of family, work, and pastimes.

Instead, most often, we deliver just the facts. "I have a beautiful wife. I've got three kids and they're awesome. My job is mostly satisfying. I love being outdoors." Sharing our faith is an essential part of who we are—the most important part!

Introducing the subject can be as simple as telling our neighbors about what God is doing in our lives, or sharing a Bible verse, or a truth that's played a significant role in our understanding of ourselves and others, or perhaps inviting them to join us in prayer because we believe in a God who listens.

Is it possible that these things will lead to complex conversations about God, the Bible, and Christianity as a whole? Sure. Is it likely our neighbors might not have the greatest reaction to our faith? You bet. Both of these reactions are possible.

But you don't need to worry about what a conversation down the road might look like. God will give you wisdom for those times as they come. On the flip side, what if your neighbor is encouraged by what you share? What if they have a genuine interest in knowing how to follow Jesus?

What if they'd like to pile into the minivan with you and your family next Sunday? As a first step, think about how you can simply share who God is to you, and what your faith means to you in your everyday life.

Of course, there are many ways to share your faith without words at all. Sharing your faith by loving your neighbors, listening to your neighbors, and serving your neighbors can often speak the loudest of all. Let Jesus be on display in your life, and people will want to know more about him. Remember, the Gospel changes everything when it comes to community: We are able to serve others freely—not out of duty, but from a place of joy.

TYING IT ALL TOGETHER

If you need a place to start when reaching out to your neighbors, practicing the BLESS strategy is a simple way to get going. The beauty of it is that there is absolutely nothing you need to start with Step 1. Simply pray for your neighbors! Asking God to lead you on the right path is the best way to begin thinking differently about those around you. Do this, and God will open your eyes and your heart.

But whatever strategy you employ (we have more simple, fun ideas for you in Chapter 7), the most important thing you can do is try. Give it a shot. Fear so often prevents us from experiencing amazing things in our lives.

Can you identify the fear that may be holding you back? Don't get stuck in the "how," but instead remember the "why." When you step out of your comfort zone and move toward those around you, stay focused on the possibilities. Your neighbors are likely more open to connection than you know.

THE MEANING OF LIFE

We've explored many reasons we need to create community in our lives. Still, at the root of all we've talked about is the fact that we will continue to exist in a dark and lonely world unless other human beings have real meaning in our lives.

It's clear from the pages of Genesis that God created everything—including you and me—for a very specific and beautiful purpose. And throughout the story of Scripture, we can see God continuing to work in and through his creation in amazing, surprising ways.

Here's the truth. Without God, our lives are trivial, meaningless, and without direction. And that's exactly what most people on this Earth are experiencing—complete nothingness! They are living for jobs, money, popularity, success, comfort, human relationships—and on and on the list goes. The reality is that none of this has eternal value. Of paramount importance in a believer's life is God's creation, his story, and his work.

One of the most powerful books you'll ever read is *Man's Search for Meaning* by Viktor Frankl. Read it—now!

The first half of the book vividly describes Frankl's harrowing experience living in a Nazi concentration camp at the end of World War II. I admit, it's difficult to read, but worth it. His observations of life and humanity, even in the worst of conditions, is riveting.

In the second half of the book, Frankl introduces his theory known as Logotherapy—the therapeutic approach of helping people find meaning in their lives. Frankl argues (and his research supports) the idea that the most important thing in life is to be healthy and happy—not wealthy, successful, or even comfortable. The most critical thing we can experience as human beings is real day-to-day meaning—to recognize our lives as worthwhile and purposeful.

As Frankl writes, "What matters, therefore, is not the meaning of life in general, but rather the specific meaning of a person's life at a given moment." In other words, it's not just about having some overarching or spiritual belief of the meaning of life as a whole, but rather having the ability to see your individual life, and the moments in it, as having significance.

The book cites many examples of this theory, and time and time again, Frankl finds that those who see their lives as having meaning are far healthier, happier, and more motivated.

"Happiness cannot be pursued," Frankl writes, "it must ensue. One must have a reason to be happy."

What are the markers of a meaningful life? Frankl identifies a few from his perspective. He believes that creating meaningful work, taking part in a significant deed, or having a project or something to build upon gives a person real meaning.

Another marker is the ability to overcome difficulty and suffering—to embrace personal growth. It is when someone is going through difficulty, but chooses to walk through it faithfully and courageously (as Frankl did during his internment at Auschwitz), that meaning can be found.

There's another thing he identifies as necessary to our meaning and purpose in life? You guessed it— relationships, or, as Frankl says, "experiencing something or encountering someone; in other words, meaning can be found not only in work, but also in love."

Moving toward another person, helping another person, serving another person—these are some of the most practical and effective ways to find meaning on this Earth, Frankl says. Meeting, knowing, understanding, and interacting with others is a pathway to a healthier and happier life.

"Really?" you might be thinking. "Most of my relationships seem to create unhappiness, stress, and conflict. I think I might need fewer relationships!" We get it. Relationships are hard. But as we've discussed, this is exactly why we need humility and optimism. This is why we need to remember that we find our ultimate security and joy in Jesus.

Most of us could use a push beyond the comfortable—beyond the surface-level, social media bubble and self-protective norm—in order to connect with those around us. To find meaning and purpose, we need to build meaningful and purposeful relationships. We have to be willing to take some risks, to put ourselves out there, in order to know others and to be known by them.

It's not just meaning in our own lives that is at stake. In a culture that is sick with loneliness, we have an incredible gift to give our neighbors—a sense of value and purpose as human beings.

Ultimately, our hope and desire is to see people come to know the love of Jesus, and experience the salvation and grace that can only be found through him. A relationship with God is the truest form of meaning and purpose. Remember, that's where it all begins—with knowing that the God of the universe wanted and created community with you.

Now God wants to use you—yes you!—to plant those seeds of community in others. You have the power to remind your neighbors, friends, coworkers, classmates, family members, and countless others, that they are seen, heard, valued, and loved. If they feel it from you, they may just begin to believe that it could be true of God as well.

STORIES FROM THE FRONT

Ty: I have a memory of one of my high school teachers that we all can learn from.

To give some context, I was educated in the public school system, and my high school was a large building with 1000 students roaming the locker-lined halls each day. Between our class periods, each of us had about five minutes to make our way to the next class. Often, it was five minutes of craziness, which stopped abruptly when the bell rang.

Many things can happen during a period of five minutes, but in some ways, those five minutes between classes were pretty predictable. Some students were always getting into trouble, while others flew under the radar, preferring not to make eye contact. If you were like me, you took full advantage of that time to breathe the same air as your high school crush. (I eventually married mine!)

The teachers played a big role during that time. One particular teacher sticks out in my mind. My Anatomy teacher had a great sense of humor and utilized his space and time to the max. Sometimes, he did extra-special things, like putting his pet bird on his shoulder and dressing up like Captain Jack Sparrow (which made most of us smile). He would also play his favorite Jock Jams CD, or the latest U2 album loud enough to

---

be heard all the way down the hall. Most notably, he was always calling kids by name and giving high fives. That Anatomy teacher, by the way, was my dad. (And, yes, he did give the "birds and bees" lesson to me, my friends, and my eventual wife.)

The lesson learned is simple. Don't waste the opportunity to connect with those around you—even if it's for only five minutes. Be present. Be creative. Be yourself. Just be there. It will make all the difference.

YOUR INNER HIGHLAND

Remember that Highland on the cover? Yeah, those funky animals can't help but make you smile, right? And they prove an important point. It doesn't take much to put a smile on someone's face. It doesn't take much to spark joy in our world. All it takes is a little optimism. All it takes is a little humility. All it takes is opening our lives to those around us in small and practical ways. All it takes is you.

God has created you to be in community—to have a deep and meaningful relationship with him and with others. It's what you were made for.

Though these relationships have been fractured by sin, and crippled by a fallen world full of challenges, the good news is that the Gospel allows us to redefine and remake that community, one courageous step at a time.

God has invited us to a party. You've been welcomed to attend. Now you can invite others to join you. You can give people a taste of the ultimate, epic one-day party to be found in Heaven by throwing a little party of your own in the here and now. And the beauty of throwing a party is that it can be anything you want it to be. You want confetti? Go for it. Balloons? Absolutely. Chocolate cake? Yep. Pie? Definitely. Chocolate cake and pie? All the better?

All that's required is that you make it meaningful. What has God placed in your heart and life that can be used to connect with those around you? Ask yourself, "What is it about me that makes others smile, laugh, or feel loved?"

Your laughter?

Your storytelling?

Your baking skills?

Your hospitality?

Your handiness?

Your sense of adventure?

Your ability to listen?

Your front porch swing?

Your electric lawn mower?

Your pets?

Your kids?

Your home?

Your heart?

Your Jesus?

We believe that each of us has exactly what we need to begin eliminating the barriers that separate us from the people who live steps away. We believe that even the smallest of steps can make a huge difference. We believe that as you make your way toward others, you'll be amazed at what God has accomplished in their lives—and in yours.

We believe that community is both possible and powerful.

What are you waiting for?

Let's push beyond the walls of our broken world.

Let's move toward others and help them discover meaning, purpose, joy, and hope.

Let's allow Jesus to lead us to the people and places He knows to be best for us.

Let's offer to the world the only true antidote for loneliness.

Let's restore community in style, right where we live.

Let's get this party started.

CHAPTER 7

GET THE PARTY STARTED

"You don't have to see the whole staircase, just take the first step." Martin Luther King, Jr.

────────── STORIES FROM THE FRONT ──────────

Ty: When I was in college, I came across a story that has stuck with me.

A fireman was going into the woods after a recent wildfire when he came to an area of the forest that had been charred. At the base of a tree, he noticed a hen that had been burned, and died as a result. As he was walking away, he heard chirping sounds. When he again approached the hen, out came a brood of chickens that had been protected from the fire by the hen's wings.

Fast forward to the spring following college and graduate school—I was finally through! It was during that same spring that I experienced God's grace through the dusty old dairy cow on the farm. I wasn't yet working a 9 to 5 job, so I was able to slow down and explore that farm on a fairly regular basis. It was the type of exploring we often did as children. No agenda required—just the pleasant experience of being carefree and expectant.

One day, I was walking around on the front lawn when I came across one of the family's hens. To my amazement, as I got closer, there were about 10 little chicks that popped their heads out from under the hen's wings.

At that moment, I remembered the story of the hen and the fireman. I smiled and thanked Jesus for the opportunity to now see the many ways in which that story—that simple little story—was a representation of my own life.

I had been living day to day feeling exposed and vulnerable because of my pride, and how I was continually hurting those closest to me. Satan isolated me in those dark days. I wasn't loving my neighbors well. Nor was I able to receive love from those around me. Life felt like a wildfire in a forest, dangerous and damaging.

But God was in the midst of it all, and He was gracious with me. So when I came across that mother hen, He reminded me that I could once again walk outside unashamed. He had blanketed me with his love and mercy, and surrounded me with people who loved and cared for me. He had allowed me to reclaim my identity and security, freeing me to start loving others well.

Jesus will forever be my blanket and protection. His conquering of sin and death once and for all through his death and resurrection resulted in the deliverance of life. And life invites us, by its very nature, to love others. And I pray that all of God's people during times like this will walk authentically and unafraid in the face of God's design for each of us. The world needs it. The world needs you.

May we party onward—and upward—for his glory!

NEW PRIORITIES

Okay, what's next? Now that you're ready to get the party started in your neighborhood, we've got some practical suggestions for you.

As you begin to move toward building community right where you are, you'll realize that your success is dependent upon one thing—priorities. What we prioritize truly does show us what matters most in our lives.

Our encouragement to you is this. Give some serious thought to the idea of how neighbors can find a place on your priority list.

Some questions to ask:

- Do you believe that God has placed you exactly where you are, in your specific part of the world, for a reason?

- Think about all the people you know. Who have you already influenced in any way, or created relationships with?

- Who in your neighborhood might be struggling with isolation or oneliness?

- What might you have to offer to begin to build community?

As we pay attention to the people around us, our priorities begin to shift. We begin to really see, hear, and care about them—not because we have to, but because we want to.

We start to see them as we see ourselves—created in the image of God. We are all humans calling out for love and care—or perhaps just for someone who will really listen, or offer a shoulder to lean on.

When we take the time to get to know our neighbors, we become aware of their struggles and burdens, and we are given an opportunity to share these experiences with them, whether in a tangible way, or by simply being there.

Think of the impact you could make in your own sphere of influence, and begin with the simplest step—prayer.

Our vision and hope is that *Party in the Front!* becomes not only a book, but a movement. We long to see more people take seriously the epidemic of loneliness in our world, and to work on enriching their lives by creating community right where they are.

If we really are made for community (and we are), and if loneliness is as threatening to our health and well-being as we now know it to be, then we have no time to waste. There are very few things you can do that are as impactful to the world around you as reaching out to your neighbors.

You can make a difference. You can be a part of this movement. We're here to cheer you on.

This chapter provides you with great practical and fun ideas to begin connecting—right now.

As you read through these proven suggestions, treat the experience like a giant brainstorming session. Highlight those you like, and cross off the ones that aren't a fit. Make notes of your own ideas.

And keep coming back to it. If one thing doesn't seem to work, try something else. Always remember that each of your neighbors has had different life experiences which, in turn, have influenced their likes, dislikes, and very distinct personalities. So what draws one person in may be a total turn-off to someone else.

The point here is to try. To begin moving toward others—and, of course, to have some fun while doing it.

I mean, what's a party without fun, right?

SIMPLE PARTY IN THE FRONT IDEAS

Spend time on your front porch. Just like Grampy Don, there is power in simply being available. Make a point to be out in front of your home for at least a few minutes each day. It's a great way to make connections.

Roll your griddle or grill out front and eat breakfast or dinner with others. Pancakes, bacon, and eggs are easy to prepare on the griddle! We like to say "If you griddle it, they will come!"

Here is a simple invitation that we've used ourselves: "Hi, we're hosting a pancake breakfast again this Saturday from 8-9:45am. Please RSVP by Wednesday. We will provide pancakes, bacon, and eggs—cooked on the griddle. Hope to see you there!"

Buy or make a picnic table and put it in the front yard. What if you started eating some of your meals in the front yard? Sure, it might feel strange at first, but that's kind of the point. People walking or driving by will almost certainly notice, and you're bound to strike up a conversation or two—or more. Cook extra food, and invite those who make contact to join you or grab something to go.

Play basketball or roller hockey in your driveway. "Game on!" Invite people to join you for a game. Sports can be a phenomenal connector of people. (Just don't trash talk too much.)

Have a yard sale. It's one of the sure-fire, time-tested events that's guaranteed to bring life to the neighborhood. You'll meet so many neighbors simply because they come to peruse your items. Make it an even more attractive event by offering refreshments.

Take your dog for a walk. One of the greatest connectors of people is dogs. People love dogs, and dogs need walks. Interaction with your neighbors is guaranteed—if you let your canine lead the way.

Bring lawn chairs out front and invite others to join you. Bonus points if you have a portable fire pit to gather around!

Do your yard work without AirPods. We love music, Podcasts, and audiobooks, too. But having headphones in definitely limits interactions with neighbors. Forget distractions for a little while, and pay attention to your surroundings.

Ask a neighbor for a cup of sugar or an egg. (If you run out of ingredients while cooking, chances are your neighbors do, too.) Then offer to return the favor—like old times—which will broaden the level of comfort in your neighborhood.

Bake your neighbor something delicious. Taking some fresh-baked cookies or muffins to someone is an awesome way to introduce yourself or let someone know you're thinking of them. Bonus points if they gave you the sugar or eggs!

Build a bike ramp. We have friends who set up a bike ramp in the front yard and invited the neighbor kids to come over and launch. It ended up being a block party, with the adults hanging out together, watching their kids get air—safely, of course.

Host a neighborhood Nerf battle. Get the word out. Set up with as many Nerf guns as you can. And let the fun begin. You'll find that both kids and adults will have a blast.

Use your garage as a neighborhood hangout. Yes, you may have to move out the junk first, but it could be a win, win, win! Just think: we're redeeming the garage, your spouse will be happy, and this new living space provides some natural shelter.

SEASONAL PARTY IN THE FRONT IDEAS

Spring/Summer Ideas:

Host a popsicle night for your neighborhood. Put some signs or flyers out, or just use word of mouth. Fill a cooler with popsicles and watch the neighborhood kids (and adults) come running. It's simple, cost-effective, and a ton of fun.

Make a lemonade stand. This is a classic and easy way to party in the front. Who doesn't love stopping at a lemonade stand staffed by cute kids?

Mow your neighbor's lawn or pull some weeds. Helping with a neighbor's yard chores is always appreciated. Bonus points if you still have an electric mower with an extension cord, like Ty's! We do recommend, however, asking your neighbor first.

Plant a communal garden. If your neighborhood already has such a space, all the better. If not, create one in your own yard. Invite folks to help you plant, maintain, and harvest the garden throughout the spring and summer.

Watch fireworks together. When the Fourth of July comes around, take advantage of it. If you can see your town's fireworks from where you live, invite your neighbors to bring over lawn chairs and watch with you. Offer some snacks or simple beverages to make it more fun. Or, if you prefer to set off your own fireworks, invite others to join you (if it's legal, of course). It could be the Superbowl of front yard hospitality for you and your neighbors.

Fall/Winter Ideas:

Bob for apples. Set up a plastic tub or a kids pool, fill it with water and apples, and invite people to share in this fun (and often hilarious) activity.

Shovel your neighbor's driveway if you live in an area that experiences a real winter. To an elderly or less mobile neighbor, this act of service will speak volumes.

Invite your neighbors over for S'mores. Consider transforming your front yard ala Dude Dad. Google "Dude

Dad Front Patio Transformation" or tune in to Dude Dad's YouTube channel.

Kick off the fall with some Funk. Have a September 21st party. Remember Earth, Wind and Fire's classic September? Introduce it to your kids. Turn up the music. Celebrate with food. You can't help but have a great time. Ty's brother and sister-in-law have been hosting a September 21st party for years.

Host a hot chocolate bar on Halloween night. Include whipped topping, sprinkles, or whatever you like. The hot chocolate bar has been a terrific hit in our neighborhood. It's a great way for everyone's kids to enjoy the evening while you engage with the parents.

Build a snowman. When was the last time you made a snowman in your front yard? It's a fun way to share your joy, and spark conversation. If you want to go above and beyond, accessorize your snowman with buttons, a scarf, and/or a fun hat. Add a sign that invites your neighbors to embellish your snowman in any way they like.

Deliver Christmas cookies and/or Christmas cards to neighbors. Many of us spend time during the Christmas season sending cards to our friends and family. It's a great tradition, but why not order extra cards to hand deliver to your neighbors? Take some Christmas treats along with you, and wish them a Merry Christmas.

TAKE OUR FRONT PORCH CHALLENGE

If you're looking for a practical place to start, try our front porch challenge. Here's how it works:

- 🎉 Sit on your front porch or stoop five nights in a row, for at least 15 minutes—without your phone. Be open to all interactions.

- 🎉 If you live in an apartment or condo where this is not possible, spend the same amount of time in your complex's common area. Set up a lawn chair in front of your building. Or laze under a tree within sight of the entryway. Take along a good book to read. That in itself may be a conversation starter..."hey, whatcha reading?"

- 🎉 Have some coffee or cookies set out to offer to those who stop to chat.

- 🎉 Make notes immediately afterward to help you remember faces, names, and subjects that came up during the conversation.

ENCOURAGE YOUR CHURCH TO REACH OUT TO THE COMMUNITY

We believe the church can be a powerful force in building community. Here are some ideas to get your church involved in this mission.

- 🎉 Talk to your pastor or ministry leaders about existing outreach opportunities in your area.

- 🎉 Lead a group on a "serving day" tour to bless neighbors in need.

- 🎉 Read a good outreach book, and share your ideas for action with your church membership.

- 🎉 Create a needs board at your church, or online, where members can share their practical needs, or those of their friends and neighbors. Then connect them to others who can help.

CONVERSATION STARTER QUESTIONS

One of the more intimidating things about meeting our neighbors is feeling like we don't know what to talk with them about. Some lucky people naturally have the gift of gab, but for others, initiating a conversation with a stranger can be terrifying.

What can help is having good ice breaker questions at the ready. It's a great way to decrease anxiety and avoid awkward silences. Use the following questions as a spring-board:

- 🎉 What are you most excited about in life right now?

- 🎉 Can you tell me about something you're currently working on?

🎉 What's your favorite thing about our neighborhood?

🎉 What's your least favorite thing about our neighborhood?

🎉 Which emoji or GIF do you most often use?

🎉 What's the most embarrassing fashion trend you used to rock?

🎉 If you could learn one new personal skill, what would it be?

🎉 What local spots would you suggest I see if I visit your hometown?

🎉 What movie, book, or show have you recently enjoyed and why?

🎉 Tell me about a career you wish you could have?

🎉 If you could wander the world, where would you like to go?

🎉 If you could have a conversation with absolutely anyone, who would it be?

🎉 What do you most look forward to doing on the weekend?

As you begin to make connections with your neighbors, remember all of the things we've talked about when it comes to connecting with the heart.

Because here's the thing: It won't always be easy. There will be times when no one stops to say hello. We've seen our daughters set up a lemonade stand and have zero—literally, zero!—customers.

It can be discouraging at times. But remember the bigger picture. Building community where you are takes time and courage. Here are some key things to remember.

PARTY IN THE FRONT'S RECIPE FOR SUCCESSFUL CONNECTIONS

🎉 Humility—Remember that God loves your neighbors as much as he loves you. Yes, even the weird ones!

🎉 Food—Remember, if you grill it, they will come. Everyone needs to eat, and good food is a great gatherer of people.

🎉 Music—Another great way to reach people is through music. Set up a Bluetooth speaker or—if you have the ability—bring a musical instrument and play some songs yourself.

🎉 Laughter—Remember, interacting with your neighbors should be an enjoyable and rewarding experience. So relax, be yourself, and have fun. People love the Highland because it's exactly who it was made to be—mess and all.

CONNECT WITH US

We would love to hear from you as you begin to pursue community in your neighborhood.

Please write to us about your experiences with connection, because every story will inspire others to share their stories of community created.

Our hope is that we will begin to see a snowball effect that has the power to battle the epidemic of loneliness in our culture.

Here's where you can find us online:

Website: partyinthefrontbook.com

Instagram: @partyinthefrontbook

Facebook: Search *Party in the Front!*

Share stories and photos on social media using: #PartyInTheFront

If you need some more help getting started, download our free guide to *Party in the Front!* Find it on Instagram, Facebook, and on our website.

RESOURCES FOR NEW CHRISTIANS

The Bridge to Life illustration is a tried-and-true resource that gives you Bible verses to explain why we need Jesus' sacrifice on the cross to solve our greatest problem—separation from God.

Find it at navigators.org/resource/the-bridge-to-life/

The New City Catechism is a modern-day resource aimed at helping children and adults learn the core doctrines of the Christian faith via fifty-two questions and answers.

Find it at newcitycatechism.com

SEE YOU AT THE PARTY

Thank you for coming on this journey with us. We hope you are encouraged and inspired to become an active participant in this movement, and to take the first step toward overcoming loneliness and building community right where you are.

We are all just beginning this exciting adventure. We can't wait to see how God supports us in taking this vision into the future.

Think of all the lonely people out there waiting to be loved and cared for.

Think of all the neighborhoods that can be transformed.

Think of all the incredible stories of relationship and connection that can be written.

Think of all the parties that are about to happen!

We look forward to hearing about it all.

Because when you take a step toward the people around you, when you let people see the real you, when you take simple actions to show love and care for your neighbors, something amazing is bound to happen.

Community happens. Relationships happen. Hope happens.

The result? A party happens. Celebrate with us.

We'll see you there.

ACKNOWLEDGEMENTS

This book was made possible by the contributions and support of so many people who helped us dream, learn and create Party in the Front!

Thank you to our wives - Becca Dillon and Ashley Dannenbring - who have supported us in this crazy adventure since day one. Thank you for allowing us to pursue this project, for encouraging us along the way, and for helping us live out the Party in the Front mission.

Thank you to our amazing kids! From the Dillon clan - Avagale, Aden Mae, Eisley, Ellie and Noah, and from the Dannenbring family - Leah, Samuel, Anna, Abigail and Joseph. You make every day a party for us. We love you!

Thank you to our parents, grandparents and extended family, who have supported us and modeled for us what it looks like to love God and love others.

Thank you to our incredible editor, Lori Johnson, who made this book start to look, feel and read like an actual book - and for making it fun and pain-free!

Thank you to Bethany Grove, whose editing and insight kept the ball rolling for us when it would have been easy to stop.

Thank you to Leif Abel, for generously helping two beginners make sense of social media and how to invite others into this movement.

Thank you to our talented team at Storybuilders for making this book even better and helping us get it across the finish line.

Thank you to Kelly Kullberg, one of our earliest supporters, who saw and supported our vision - and even tried it out in her own neighborhood!

Thank you to our friends and ministry partners at Redemption Church Loveland, The Crossing Church and the Crossway Network.

Thank you to everyone who allowed us to share their stories in this book - it's the best part of Party in the Front!

Thank you to our neighbors, who have allowed us to be imperfect, messy people - and yet still have allowed us to build community right where we are.

And finally, thank you to our Lord and Savior Jesus Christ, whose sacrificial death on the cross and resurrection from the dead gives us the hope, the motivation and the means to move toward the people around us."So if the Son sets you free, you will be free indeed." (John 8:36)

ABOUT THE AUTHORS

Jeff Dillon is a Pastor at Redemption Church in Loveland, Colorado and a journalism major from Colorado State University, where he learned his love of sharing stories through writing. He and his wife Becca have five kids and love the mountains, traveling and being outside to enjoy the sunshine - and connect with their neighbors.

Ty Dannenbring is a financial advisor in Loveland, Colorado, where he strives to serve his clients with integrity and care. He grew up in South Dakota and graduated from Lenoir-Rhyne University in North Carolina. He is an avid golfer and loves connecting with people. He and his wife Ashley also have five kids and enjoy inviting neighbors over for Saturday morning pancakes.

ENDNOTES

1. Merriam-Webster.com. Merriam-Webster, 2011.

2. Office of the U.S. Surgeon General, "U.S. Surgeon General's Advisory on the Healing Effects of Social Connection and Community." 2023.

3. Library of Congress Online, "U.S. History Primary Source Timeline." Loc.gov.

4. Lasalle University. "The Urban Sprawl." Lasalle.edu.

5. Encyclopedia.com. "Bowling, Beatniks, and Bell-Bottoms: Pop Culture of 20th-Century America."

6. Putnam, Robert. Bowling Alone: The Collapse and Revival of American Community. Simon & Schuster, 2001.

7. DFT Communications. "Happy Birthday to the World Wide Web!" DFTCommunications.com.

8. GCF Global. "What is an Echo Chamber?" edu. gcfglobal.org.

9. Office of the U.S. Surgeon General, "U.S. Surgeon General's Advisory on the Healing Effects of Social Connection and Community." 2023.

10. Gallup News. "U.S. Church Membership Falls Below Majority for First Time." news.gallup.com. 2021.

11. Pew Research. "How the Pandemic Has Affected Attendance at U.S. Religious Services. PewResearch. org. 2023.

12. Jones, Jeffrey M. "U.S. Church Membership Down Sharply in Past Two Decades." news.gallup.com. 2019.

13. Reach the Lost. "Unpacking Church Attendance Statistics for 2023." reachthelost.com. 2023.

14. Austin, Jon. "How the Church Growth Movement has De-Churched Christians." The Reformed Journal, 2023.

15. Brown, Brene. The Gifts of Imperfection: Let Go of Who You Think You're Supposed to Be and Embrace Who You Are. Hazelden, 2010.

16. Psychology Today. "The Science Behind the Joy of Sharing Joy." PschologyToday.com. 2013.

17. Putnam, Robert. Bowling Alone: The Collapse and Revival of American Community. Simon & Schuster, 2001.

18. Pew Research Center. "Race in America 2019." PewResearch.org. 2019.

19. Pew Research Center. "Pew Religion and Life Survey." PewResearch.org. 2009.

20. Pew Research Center. "Where Americans Find Meaning in Life." PewResearch.org. 2017.

21. Pinsker, Joe. "'Ugh, I'm So Busy': A Status Symbol for Our Time." The Atlantic. 2017.

22. Ray, Julie. "World Unhappier, More Stressed Out than Ever." news.gallup.com. 2022.

23. Merriam-Webster.com. Merriam-Webster, 2011.

24. Pew Research Center. Partisanship and Political Animosity in 2016. PewResearch.org. 2016.

25. Holt-Lunstad, et. al. "Social Relationships and Mortality Risk: A Meta-analytic Review." doi.org. 2010.

26. Ferguson. Dave, The Verge Network. "BLESS Strategy." VergeNetwork.org.